THE
DREAM
SOURCEBOOK

THE DREAM SOURCEBOOK

A GUIDE TO THE THEORY AND INTERPRETATION OF DREAMS

BY
PHYLLIS R. KOCH-SHERAS, PH.D.
AND AMY LEMLEY

Lowell House
Los Angeles

Contemporary Books
Chicago

Copyright © 1995 by RGA Publishing Group, Inc.
All rights reserved. No part of this work may be reproduced or transmitted in any form or by any means, electronic or mechanical, including photocopying or recording, or by any information storage or retrieval system, except as may be expressly permitted by the 1976 Copyright Act or in writing by the Publisher.

Requests for such permissions should be addressed to:
Lowell House
2029 Century Park East, Suite 3290
Los Angeles, CA 90067

Lowell House books can be purchased at special discounts when ordered in bulk for premiums and special sales. Contact Department JH at the address above.

Publisher: Jack Artenstein
General Manager, Lowell House Adult: Bud Sperry
Text Design: Laurie Young
ISBN 1-56565-336-X
Manufactured in the United States of America

To my parents, who always had a dream for me
    —Phyllis Koch-Sheras

To my sister, whose dreams I'll always share
    —Amy Lemley

ACKNOWLEDGMENTS

Writing a book, like dreamwork, is a collaborative process. Not only between us as co-authors, but also among the friends, family, clients, colleagues, and members of our community with whom we have talked about this project. To all of you who shared our questions and suggested answers, thank you for your contributions to this project. We especially want to acknowledge those who so graciously and openly shared their dream experiences for this book, including Richard Abidin, Ian Clark, E. Ann Hollier, Karla Scappini, and Sharon Davie. We also want to thank the reference librarians at the Jefferson-Madison Regional Library in Charlottesville for their patience, help, and support while doing research for the book.

Phyllis Koch-Sheras wishes to thank her dream guides and teachers John and Joyce Weir, John and Anna Koehne, Stanley Krippner, Leonard Tuchyner, Henry Reed, and Helen Ammons. Last but not least, she thanks her husband Peter Sheras and their children Daniel and Sarah for their patience and support during the hard times and always.

Amy Lemley wishes to thank Freyda Epstein, Jon Fink, Laura and Norman Lemley, Chuck Lewis, Sharon Marshall, Jane Lemley Rasmussen, and Gabe Silverman for giving her the chance to live various dreams. In life, as in dreams, a single gesture, small or large, can be symbolic and transformative. Thank you all.

CONTENTS

INTRODUCTION
DARING TO DREAM
AN INVITATION TO ENTER A NEW WORLD ✵ XI

CHAPTER ONE
WHAT'S IN A DREAM?
WHAT WE THINK AND WHAT WE KNOW ✵ 1

CHAPTER TWO
DREAMS THROUGH TIME
A HISTORY OF DREAMS IN VARIOUS CULTURES ✵ 23

CHAPTER THREE
MODERN DREAM THEORISTS
WHO SAYS WHAT ABOUT DREAMS ✵ 47

CHAPTER FOUR
A SYMBOL IS WORTH A THOUSAND WORDS
WHAT YOUR DREAMS MAY BE TELLING YOU ✵ 75

CHAPTER FIVE
WHAT'S IT ALL MEAN?
A GUIDE TO RECALLING AND INTERPRETING
YOUR DREAMS ✵ 109

CHAPTER SIX
MAKING YOUR DREAMS YOUR FRIENDS
EXERCISES IN DREAM EXPLORATION ✵ 135

CHAPTER SEVEN
SLEEPING ON IT
USING DREAMS TO ENHANCE YOUR CREATIVITY,
PRODUCTIVITY, AND HEALING ✵ 171

CHAPTER EIGHT
COINCIDENCE? MAYBE
PSYCHIC PHENOMENA AND DREAMS ✵ 193

CHAPTER NINE
DREAMWORK TEAMWORK
SHARING YOUR DREAMS ✵ 209

APPENDIX A
BIBLIOGRAPHY ✵ 231

APPENDIX B
INDEX ✵ 241

INTRODUCTION

DARING TO DREAM
AN INVITATION TO
ENTER A
NEW WORLD

Imagine sitting down with an expert who could help you to discover all you want to know about your dreams: where they might come from, why you might have them, what they might mean, and how you could use them to enrich your life—personally, professionally, and spiritually. This expert would place this knowledge right at your fingertips, allowing you access every time you had a question or desire to learn more about a dream.

Imagine that *you* are that expert.

This idea is not as unusual as it sounds. After all, who knows you more than you know yourself? *The Dream Sourcebook: A Guide to the Theory and Interpretation of Dreams* features *you* as the source of your own dream world. Throughout this book, as we explore the myths and facts about dreams, dream physiology, the place of dreams in different cultures, the interpretation of dream symbols, and the relation of dreams to psychic phenomena, we present a broad perspective that enables you to apply these many theories and ideas to your own dream experiences. In the final chapters, we offer opportunities to use your dreams: to interpret and adapt them in ways that enhance your creative mind, increase your waking productivity, ease your troubled psyche, improve your physical well-being, and build a connection with the world community through shared dreamwork. Your dreams, then, become your teachers, educating you on the subject of yourself and training you to become the expert authority on your own desires, fears, conflicts, and joys.

Too many times we underestimate ourselves as experts and specialists, ignore our instincts and abilities, and instead look to other authorities who appear to know more, seem to be better educated, or are just more vocal with their opinions. But now, with *The Dream Sourcebook* as a personal consultant, you can acquire the tools you need to become your own expert, to trust your knowledge and interpretation of your own dreams. After all, an expert is not someone who fails to consult outside resources, but rather someone who knows what resources are available and how to use them. Experts are not afraid to ask questions or request assistance. They admit what they don't know and are committed to discovering the answers.

So many people share a love of dreamwork, the process of recalling and exploring dreams. They know that the world of dreams is both fun, and inspiring: Not only does it provide topics for some engaging conversation, but it also offers a chance for increased self-knowledge and enhanced creativity. Novice dreamworkers will find here all they need to enter the world of dreams. And because *The Dream Sourcebook* is intended to serve as a comprehensive reference book for all dreamers, we have designed it so that experienced dreamworkers, too, will find much to work with. Think of this book as a map for finding your way to yourself as your own source of truth. If you are new to the world of dreaming, you might use this map to view the general lay of the land, venturing down various streets and avenues simply to see where they lead. If you have spent years learning from your dreams, you might refer to this map when you wish to return to a particular destination, to discover fellow dream travelers from various times and places, or perhaps to learn more about specific methods of transportation—such as translating a dream narrative into dream language, establishing and working with dream groups, and dream incubation—to get you there.

Why become an expert on your dreams? There are several reasons. First, your dreaming mind has access to information about yourself that is not readily available to your waking mind. As adults, and even as children and adolescents, we rely on a complex combination of skills to experience our worlds; as a result, we may become distracted or burdened by the many aspects of life we have to factor in at any one time. Our dreams can help us sort through the debris of our lives and clean house psychologically, whether we consciously pay attention to their content or not. Of course, knowing where the "dirt" is points the way for psychic housecleaning where you need it most. And that's what dreams often do: highlight issues in need of attention, resolution, or closure.

Researchers have identified what are called "peak experiences," those occurrences in which you are totally focused on what you are doing and feeling at the moment: watching a breathtaking sunset, listening to a beautiful piece of music. Peak experiences have demonstrably positive effects on the body, mind, and spirit. This level of intensity, enrichment, and joy is rare, and peak experiences are very few. In our dreams, we are not judging, we are not thinking, we are not figuring out, we are just creating and experiencing. Every night, our dreams offer the opportunity for a peak experience, and all of the positive effects that kind of experience can bring.

So it is the dreaming mind that can probe the deeper level of ourselves, of our souls, to explore what psychologist and dream expert Ann Faraday calls the "thoughts of the heart." The dreaming mind can see beyond the conscious mind, revealing to us, without prejudice, our underlying motivations, our desires and fears. Indeed, some studies show that your mind functions more fully when it is dreaming than when it is awake: "Brain wave records indicate that the dreaming brain is even more active than the waking brain," Faraday writes in *Dream Power,* "which may mean that it is capable of more work in a given amount of time. Computer experts would say that more information per unit time is being 'processed' by the brain."

Is there a way to harness that brain power? We think so. Your dreaming mind is able to sort out the day's events, to categorize them and interpret them in ways your waking mind may not. Perhaps this function explains why most dreams are related to events from the previous day or two. How necessary is this function? Although dreams may seem frivolous to the untrained dreamer, they are anything but. In fact, your thinking and memory skills and your physical and emotional well-being all depend on dreaming. Studies on dream deprivation show that people who are denied their dream time may suffer impaired functioning in a matter of days, possibly becoming disoriented and even depressed. You could go without food and water for several days longer than you could go without dreaming.

Have you ever awakened from a dream with a clear solution to something that had puzzled you before? Many of us have, and these experiences are further evidence that our brains keep working even as we rest our bodies. The symbols that appear in our dreams contain messages to us, messages we have created ourselves. The dreaming mind is like a movie director, who uses images of sight and sound (and, in the case of dreams, smell, touch, and taste) to convey meaning. No, dreams do not always tell cohesive stories—and some of them do seem strange or nonsensical. But we can often find a way to make some sense of them, and in doing so, learn more about ourselves.

In giving us this unique picture of ourselves, our dreams provide healing power. A dream unifies body, mind, and spirit—the doing, thinking, and feeling parts of us—in one free-flowing experience that is our essential truth. Dreams can bring up information from our unconscious to offer our waking minds a kind of prompt for action, pointing out physical conditions or deficiencies we can then correct in our waking lives: marking the anniversary of a death or other important event, or urging us to confront our fears by allowing us a metaphorical "practice session" during sleep, to cite some examples. For example, one woman reported the following experience: "About five weeks after I swallowed a small chicken bone, my throat was still sore. I had the sensation that the bone was still there. In a dream I had during that time, I have cancer and am refusing treatment. The dream pointed out to me that I was avoiding my problem and should seek some medical relief. The next day, I contacted my doctor, who gave me a prescription that eliminated the throat irritation in a week."

> "A DREAM IS LIKE A PERSONAL DOCUMENT, A LETTER TO ONESELF."
> —Calvin Hall, dream research pioneer

Dreams can give us the information we need; we have only to recognize it. Using this book as your map, you will find many paths to follow and discover what only you will recognize once you arrive there—the truth as it connects with your own experience. This map can take you there, but only you can go to the source of your own truth.

The field of psychology has long recognized the value of looking within to discover strength and clarity, and current therapies and personal growth programs make use of dreams as a revealing pathway. But even cultures with no knowledge of psychology per se have made use of dreams, as chapter 2 reveals. Whether ancient or contemporary, dreamwork offers a chance to achieve great insight and inner peace through self-exploration.

This opportunity is partly what has kept co-author Phyllis Koch-Sheras, an experienced dreamworker, interested in dreams, both personally and professionally. She writes:

> I have found that thinking about my dreams first thing in the morning brings focus to my entire day, especially if I wake up tired or feeling under the weather. If I take a few minutes to write down my dream, I have more energy for the waking day. In addition to working on my dreams alone, working on them with others—friends, family members, colleagues, and groups—has really opened up the power of dreams to me and motivated me to write about them.

> After reading Fritz Perls' Gestalt Therapy Verbatim shortly after it came out, I started using his innovative dreamwork techniques to teach child care workers in a state hospital how to understand and help the very disturbed children they worked with every day. The insight, progress, and peace we achieved by applying Perls' ideas were remarkable.

> Learning more about the power of dreams in workshops on self-differentiation with personal

growth leaders John and Joyce Weir reinforced my commitment to continue working on and sharing my dreams in my daily life. It was around this same time that I started meeting regularly with a friend to work on our dreams. Seventeen years later, that friend and I still get together every other week to share our dreams and help each other explore them. Chapter 9 describes in detail this valuable experience—and how you can create it for yourself.

More than a decade ago, the enthusiasm of two women who attended a talk I gave about dreams led to our co-writing Dream On: A Dream Interpretation and Exploration Guide for Women. *(Prentice-Hall, 1983). These dedicated dreamers, E. Ann Hollier and Brooke Jones, brought their own dreamwork experiences to the table and, as a result, we learned an incredible amount from each other and from the many women whose dreams we included. By studying the dreamwork of researchers and practitiioners over the centuries, I have come to feel a sense of community and support for my own dream process. In the course of writing this book and presenting dream workshops, I have found that the more I work on my dreams and share my dreamwork techniques, the more I learn about myself, expand my consciousness, and contribute to others—all beyond my wildest dreams!*

Besides offering a chance for personal growth, dreamwork is fun—which is perhaps the reason most of us become interested in dreams to begin with. For co-author Amy Lemley, a journalist and novice dreamworker, the pleasure of sharing and deciphering dreams is what made this book project appealing:

I have always been a vivid dreamer, and would usually regale—or sometimes bore—my friends and family with my dreams each morning. Sometimes a dream or dream fragment would seem to have a particular meaning for me, but I never knew quite how to play around with the characters, objects, and events in order to pinpoint the most accurate interpretation. Until we began this book, the reporter in me thought it was up to the experts to tell me what my dreams meant. But now I understand that I am the real expert when it comes to interpreting my own dreams.

As we proceeded chapter by chapter, my dreams worked right along with us. As I was learning about dream helpers, those dream characters who seem all-seeing or all-knowing, a dream helper would appear in a dream. As I was writing about nightmares, I had the first (and worst) nightmare I had had in a very long time. When it came time to learn about finishing and changing dreams, my dreams presented themselves as perfect guinea pigs. It's true what they say: Simply by paying more attention to your dreams—by acknowledging them as the friends they really are to you—you can gain an immeasurable amount of insight and pleasure, and achieve real personal growth. These days, it is not unusual for me to recall in great detail as many as five dreams a night, simply by following some of the procedures we outline in this book. And whether I simply speak them aloud, write them down, or share them with others, these dreams offer much to think about, to laugh about, and to learn from.

The symbol language our dreams speak to us is like a puzzle to solve, and the reward for our efforts is a deeper understanding of ourselves and how we think and feel. Although we will give you several suggested meanings for dream symbols, we do not believe a "dream dictionary" with page after page of symbols and their meanings would be sufficient to give you the expertise you need to understand your dreams. It is up to you to use the suggestions in this sourcebook to develop your own personal dictionary of what your dream symbols mean to you. We can offer suggestions—that a bird might symbolize freedom, for example, or an oak tree strength—but it's up to you to decide whether these possibilities are relevant for you. No two people have had exactly the same life experience, and so no two people will interpret a symbol the exact same way. As with any other language, the more you practice dream language, the more fluent you will become.

There is no one right way to work with your dreams, just as there is no one correct interpretation of a dream. This book offers a cross section of what researchers, theorists, and people of various cultures have thought about dreams over the centuries. We also offer the dreamwork techniques that have been most popular and successful over the years. But it is up to you to choose your own path, to discover your own route on the map, to lead yourself to your source through the study of your dreams.

As for the dreaming itself, simply knowing a little more about how and why you dream can open a whole new world of consciousness for you, a world you can remember, a world filled with dream helpers and dream symbols and dream landscapes. You'll discover a world in which you can spend time with those you love, living or dead, remember forgotten people, places, and events from the past, visit places exotic and familiar, have intimate contact with famous figures from the past or present, confront enemies and triumph over danger, and so much more.

You spend about a third of your life sleeping. And you dream more than a thousand times a year—whether you remember your dreams or not. By the time you turn seventy, you will have spent about six years of your life in Dreamland. Make the most of it. Dare to dream!

THE
DREAM
SOURCEBOOK

CHAPTER ONE

WHAT'S IN A DREAM?
WHAT WE THINK
AND WHAT
WE KNOW

What is a dream? Is it a story that evolves in your mind, all in a single flash, moving from start to finish in seconds? Why do you dream more vividly one night than another? Was it spicy food eaten late at night? And those fragmented images you imagine just as you are falling asleep—are those dreams or merely thoughts? When does a dream become a nightmare?

To begin with, we need to establish some common terminology, so that we are speaking the same language about dreams. The word *dream* appears in many expressions: "dreamy" and "dreamland" and "dream up," "dream house" and "dream boat" and "dream lover," "hopes and dreams" and Martin Luther King, Jr.'s "I have a dream." A dream holds power, promise, and inspiration.

Webster's New World Dictionary defines the word *dream* in five ways: first, as "a sequence of sensations, images, thoughts, etc., passing through a sleeping person's mind"; second, as "a fanciful vision, a fantasy"; third, as "a state of reverie"; fourth, as "a fond hope or aspiration"; and fifth, as "anything so lovely, charming, transitory, etc., as to seem dreamlike."

Indeed, any of these definitions rings true for us as dreamers. Linguists say the Modern English language word *dream* is derived from the Middle English *dreem* or *dreme*, which harkens back to the Old English word *dream*, meaning "joy" and "music" or "noise," and also to the Old Norse *draumr*, meaning "dream" (which is related to the Old High German *troum*, which also means "dream").

Centuries ago, people in many cultures believed dreams were presented by an outside force and intended to serve as oracles or omens. Later, people theorized that dreams were caused by anxiety, household noises, and even indigestion. Dreaming is certainly a mysterious process: Images float by, often at lightning speed, improbable events seem commonplace, people from our past emerge, people we have never met become our close friends or bitter enemies. A concentrated effort in dream research since 1952 has netted some concrete results, enabling us to define dreaming as a psychophysiological (or mind-body) process and to begin to understand the role dreams play in basic human functioning. The prevailing notion, based on psychological research and scientific study, is that dreams are our own inventions, born of a mind that remains fully active—with brain waves racing and five senses perceiving—even as we slumber in relative physical calm. Here is the definition that scientific research has given us: A dream is a period of spontaneous brain activity usually lasting from about five to forty minutes that occurs during sleep several times a night, usually at about ninety-minute intervals.

TYPES OF DREAMS

Although we will be referring throughout this book to dreams in general, it is useful to keep in mind some distinctions about particular kinds of dreams. There are several different types of dreams.

FANTASY, DAYDREAM, AND WAKING DREAM

Many people think of a fantasy as something sexual—an imagined encounter with an acquaintance, famous person, or even a stranger. Still others think of a fantasy as akin to a fairy tale, the stuff of unicorns and witches and princesses in towers. But as a psychological term, fantasy means anything your mind conjures up while awake. The fantasy may be a response to a real situation: Your new boyfriend cancels plans with you and your fantasy is that he has met someone else and is going out with her instead. Or it may be a daydream or "waking dream": You are awake, and as your mind begins to wander, you lose yourself in an imagined scenario such as winning an award, saving the president's life, or attacking your former girlfriend and her date. The content of fantasy or daydream is unrestricted, and can be positive or negative. It is like a dream in that you follow your imagination where it takes you, rather than guiding the images as you would in normal waking thought. But it differs from a dream in that you are in a waking state rather than a sleeping state while it occurs.

LUCID DREAM

Have you ever realized you were dreaming while the dream was still happening? That is what dream experts call a lucid dream. Most people have had this experience at some time, and it is often during a nightmare, when the fear of the situation suddenly lifts as you say to yourself, Wait a minute, this is only a dream! A lot of times, however, dreamers wake themselves up as soon as they notice they are dreaming. Next time it happens to you, try to stay in that state of dreaming sleep and pay attention to where your conscious dreaming takes you. (Chapter 6 outlines lucid dreaming in detail, offering techniques to cultivate this type of dream awareness.)

NIGHTMARE

We just mentioned that lucid dreams often take place during nightmares. What is a nightmare exactly? Is it different from a scary dream? Not really. A nightmare is a disturbing dream that causes the dreamer to wake up feeling anxious or frightened. The content of the dream is easily recalled, and while the plot may seem silly in the clear light of day (being pursued by a neon-colored Frankenstein, riding in a car with no wheels) the strong emotions are all too real, and may stay with the dreamer for several days.

Most people have nightmares about being chased: For children, the pursuer is usually an animal or a fantasy figure such as a monster. For adults, the pursuer is usually an unknown male figure. Nightmares also feature a kind of replay of real-life traumatic events, and are often brought on by these events. Drugs, illness, and stress all seem to contribute to the likelihood that a dreamer will have a nightmare.

> "LET NOT OUR BABBLING DREAMS AFFRIGHT OUR SOULS."
> —William Shakespeare, English dramatist and poet

But even without these factors in place, just about everyone has had a nightmare at some point in life. Nightmares are actually considered a normal part of child development, occurring frequently in children under ten, who are still learning the basics of negotiating their fears and conflicts. Grown-ups have them too, however. In fact, studies suggest that as many as one in ten adults has nightmares at least once a month, with women reporting three times as many as men do. (Both children and adults can benefit a great deal from candid discussion of the monsters in their minds; for this reason, we believe there are no "bad dreams," though some are scary or disturbing.)

NIGHT TERROR

A child wakes up in an extreme state of panic, perhaps screaming out in fear and appearing dazed. Her heart races, she perspires, and she just can't seem to calm down. She may even hallucinate. Yet when you ask her what she was dreaming about, she might not be able to remember. The only thing she knows is that she is absolutely terrified. This is a night terror. How does it differ from a nightmare? Put simply, you could say that night terrors are basically severe nightmares. They are common in children ages three to five, but can also occur in older children and adults. Research shows that nearly two-thirds of adults say they have had one night terror or more. Night terrors are more frequent in males than females, though both boys and girls usually outgrow them by adolescence. (Chapter 9 offers some tips on how to learn from their nightmares, and to cope with night terrors, which, perhaps, should be dealt with in a different way than nightmares.)

MYTHS AND FACTS ABOUT DREAMS

It has taken centuries of interest to move beyond dream lore to a scientific understanding of dreams. Yet many myths are still taken as fact in interpreting our own and others' dream behavior. Let's examine some of the more popular myths about dreaming:

MYTH: Some people dream only a few times a year—or not at all.

FACT: Everybody dreams. Everybody! While some people may only remember a few dreams a year, they actually dream several times every night, usually every hour and a half. The trouble is, many people have a hard time remembering their dreams. Even people who are able to remember part of their dreams upon wakening or at some point during the day will quickly lose that memory unless they take some steps to note their dream content, by writing it down, recording it on a cassette player, or telling it to a friend or loved one. (Chapter 6 details strategies to improve your dream recall.)

MYTH: Babies don't dream. After all, what could they have to dream about?

FACT: Babies do show evidence of dreaming, although what they dream about is anybody's guess. Even a newborn infant will have rapid eye movement or REM sleep—the kind of sleep in which we dream—most of the time. That's a lot of REM sleep, considering that babies spend twice as much time sleeping as adults do, usually about two-thirds of their day. Scientists believe there is a connection between REM sleep and brain development, citing evidence that, for instance, REM sleep occurs 80 percent of the time in an infant born ten weeks prematurely, dropping to 50 percent in the full-term baby, and 35 percent in the one-year-old. Why do babies dream so much? REM sleep may provide "nerve exercise" from within the brain for newborns until they can get more stimulation from the external environment as they get older. The trend continues as humans age. Five-year-olds dream 20 percent of the time they are sleeping, which is roughly the same as the percentage of time adults spend dreaming each night. As people continue to age, studies show, the percentage of time spent dreaming drops off to as low as 13 percent in some people.

MYTH: Animals do not dream.

FACT: As dog owners readily suspect, animals do dream. Dogs sometimes move their legs, wag their tails, and even bark and growl while sleeping. As with infants' dreams, dogs' dream content is not something we can easily discern, though some proud pet owners like to say, "Oh, he's dreaming of chasing rabbits" or "I bet she's dreaming about the mail carrier." Around the turn of the century, Sigmund Freud, the father of contemporary dream theory, wrote about animal dreams in his landmark book *The Interpretation of Dreams:* "I do not myself know what animals dream of. But a proverb . . . does claim to know. 'What,' asks the proverb, 'do geese dream of?' And it replies: 'Of maize!' The whole theory that dreams are wish fulfillments is contained in these two phrases."

But what about other animals? In all mammals studied, there is evidence of REM sleep. (Anyone with a dog or cat can observe moving eyelids during sleep, usually ten or twenty minutes after the pet falls asleep.) And scientists have sought to prove whether animals actually see images while they are sleeping. In one experiment, monkeys were trained to touch a lever whenever they received visual stimulation. Then, while they slept, the monkeys pressed the lever again, apparently in response to the visual stimulation of dreaming. What they see has yet to be determined.

MYTH: Blind people do not dream.

FACT: Blind people do dream. According to author Charles W. Kimmins, as quoted in *The New World of Dreams,* researchers have found that "all dreamers becoming blind after the age of seven see in dreams even after an interval of twenty or thirty years." Those who became blind before age five, however, almost never see in their dreams. Generally, in dreams as in waking life, a person with one impaired sense compensates with other senses. Thus, a person who cannot hear often has especially vivid visual content in dreams, and a person blind from birth distinctly remembers sounds and tactile experiences in dreams.

MYTH: There are no differences between men and women in the area of dreaming.

FACT: From the earliest days of modern dream research, scientists have documented differences in men's and women's dream recall, dream content, and dreaming patterns. Traditionally, the waking interests, goals, and personalities of men and women have differed. So it is not surprising that men's and women's dreams reflect these differences. Women tend to recall and share their dreams more often than men, perhaps because women tend to focus more on inner processes. Women also report more nightmares and more psychic dreams than men do. Research collected in the 1940s showed significant differences in the content of men's and women's dreams. But current research shows a change in these tendencies, as gender roles continue to equalize. The source of these sex differences in dreams is still unclear. As with other gender issues, the nature-nurture controversy remains: How much difference is inherent (due to our biological purposes or physiological makeups) and how much is acquired (due to the environments in which we were raised and the society in which we function)? Brain research suggests that men's and women's brains are actually organized differently: Magnetic resonance imaging has enabled researchers to observe that women use both hemispheres of the brain more than men do, giving them a broader or at least a different base than men from which to operate. This greater connection between the left and right brains, acting with hormones, could account for women's greater sensitivity to emotions and even so-called women's intuition. Given that dreams and dreamwork tap into these skill areas, this research may serve to explain women's higher level of dream recall, and their greater interest in sharing their dreams.

MYTH: People dream in black-and-white.

FACT: For those who can see, or who became blind sometime after birth, studies show that dreams take place in colors, sometimes as vivid as real life. In fact, in studies in which dreamers were awakened during the dream cycle and asked about color, the subjects could remember it 80 percent of the time. The reason so many people claim to dream in black-and-white may be that color is not as memorable to them as other aspects of the dream, so people "remember" seeing their dream in black-and-white. One dreamer, an aspiring movie director, reports that he has had a "film noir"–style dream, which appeared to be in black-and-white like a classic movie.

MYTH: Dreams take place in a flash, and what seems like hours is really only seconds.

FACT: Sleepers view dreams as though they are watching a film or experiencing an adventure story scene by scene, and they generally take as long to dream as they would to "watch" or experience. Dreams have scenes that may start and finish, skip ahead to the future, or regress to the past, sometimes giving the impression that the plot unfolds far more quickly than the dream's actual time span. As we said, there are several periods of dreaming throughout every night, and these periods get longer and longer as sleep progresses. Your final dreaming session may last as long as an hour.

MYTH: Most dreams take place as we fall asleep or wake up.

FACT: In fact, the often fleeting images we experience as we fall asleep seem an awful lot like dreams. But these hypnagogic (as you're falling asleep) and hypnomonic (as you're waking up) dreams are not so fully formed as regular dreams, consisting generally of physical sensations, snippets of words or conversations, and flashing images that may seem disjointed. Dreamlets, as they are sometimes called, do not include the rapid eye movement sleep of full-fledged dreams. And rarely do they contain enough content to be of much interest for dream interpretation.

One sometimes frustrating type of falling-asleep dreamlet is the one in which you jerk yourself awake. This is known as a myclonic jerk. Although there may be some fleeting image or experience that leads to this sensation (a feeling of slipping and falling or, in one dreamer's case, a visual image of tripping over a doorjamb), there is no full plot involved at this stage, and generally no disturbing emotions (save a fear of insomnia!) are associated with the experience.

MYTH: If you dream that you die, you may indeed die—by having a heart attack from the fear and shock the dream causes.

FACT: We think this misguided notion may reflect the fact that many people awaken as they dream of crashing a car, falling off a cliff, or otherwise endangering themselves. When you consider that nightmares are scary dreams that almost always awaken the dreamer, it seems clear that our own tendency to rouse ourselves might suggest that we are doing so to save our own lives. But never fear! There are plenty of people who have dreamed of dying only to awaken the next morning and recount the imagined ordeal over coffee and doughnuts. For example, a man reports that he has had several dreams in which he dies, and then regards himself as an observer would. "Actually," he comments, "it gets kind of boring. I am dead, and I can't get up and do anything. I just lie there. But the dream goes on."

MYTH: It is dangerous to awaken a sleepwalker or a person having a nightmare.

FACT: This misconception probably stems from bad experiences people may have had after startling a sleepwalker into consciousness: The person may have struck out in defense, or tripped and fallen. But it is not psychologically dangerous to wake a sleepwalker; and it is certainly more dangerous to let the sleeping person wander around, because he or she could get hurt. Leading a sleepwalker to a safe place, such as an uncluttered area in a room, or back to bed, is a good idea. Experts think getting the person back to bed without waking him or her is an even better one, because it may allow the person to move gently into the next stage of sleep, perhaps resolving whatever issue may have led to the nighttime restlessness of sleepwalking. A chronic problem, however, might merit medical or psychiatric attention, if only because the person might do something dangerous during sleep such as wander onto a balcony or into the street.

Sleepwalkers report having nightmares or night terrors 60 percent of the time, though sleepwalking and the dream state do not in fact coincide. Whether the person sleepwalks or not, it is best to let him or her sleep through a nightmare or night terror so as to complete the dream. If a dreamer screams out in the middle of the night, do not try to restrain or rouse the person unless it's necessary for safety. Instead, touch and speak to the person gently and soothingly, reassuring him or her that everything's all right, and you're there. Then let the dreamer return to sleep as soon as possible.

MYTH: A dream can predict the future.

FACT: Many people have had the experience of dreaming something that later, in some form or another, actually did occur. Often, this is just coincidence. Other times, the dreamer may be pulling together several strands of known information to derive a conclusion that the mind could not make while awake. Laboratory studies have focused on psychic phenomena in dreams, and have substantiated some precognitive dreams, but as yet there is no explanation of how psychic dreams (also called *psi dreams*) occur or what causes them. Chapter 8 explores these occurrences in depth.

MYTH: Dreams have no meaning.

FACT: This is the $64,000 Question: Do dreams have meaning? For most of this century, psychologists have plumbed the murky depths of patients' dreams in search of answers that the patients' conscious minds cannot offer. Dream interpretation has hit the mainstream, too, with dream workshops and interpretation groups forming in many communities throughout the United States and elsewhere.

But this has not always been the outlook regarding dreams. In the nineteenth century, scientists considered dreams the result of indigestion or anxiety, and denied that they had any meaning at all. And in centuries previous to that one, dreams were infused by meanings that were outside the control of the dreamer: Gods or demons supplied the dreams, people believed. Chapter 2 offers a history of dreams in human experience.

Interestingly, there is renewed interest in the theory that dreams are meaningless, as scientists research potential physical causes of dreaming that have nothing to do with unresolved conflicts or hidden meanings. Chapter 3 offers an overview of the many theories that form the basis of current dream thought.

Let's examine what we know about the physical nature of dreaming and how it relates to the various theories of what dreams mean. Since scientists have begun to study the phenomenon of dreaming in the laboratory, there is more conclusive evidence of the existence of dreams and how they physically occur. From this information, we can learn more about what is happening in our bodies as we dream, which may help us better understand their function and possible meaning.

"He Died in His Sleep"

Have you ever stopped to wonder just why people die in their sleep? As early as the 1920s, one doctor guessed that there might be a correlation between the sleep "disturbances" we now know to be REM sleep and the incidence of heart attack. We know today that most heart attacks during sleep occur in the early morning hours, when the longest period of REM sleep takes place. Given that heart and breathing rates increase and become more erratic during REM sleep, sometimes reaching levels not seen during waking life, it makes sense that a diseased heart might one night fail to withstand the strain. No one knows for sure whether dream content or emotion play a role in nighttime heart attack, or to what extent the heart attack is merely the result of the high physical demands of the REM period.

THE MECHANICS OF DREAMING

Your adrenaline is racing. Your blood pressure increases as your heart beats faster and faster. Your breathing becomes rapid and shallow. The final leg of a challenging foot race? Far from it.

Would you believe this is the description of your sleeping body during the dreaming stage? It's true. A 1993 study at the University of Iowa found that the human body's dreaming condition is much like the fight-or-flight response in waking life, which gears the body up to confront a threatening situation. Yet your brain simultaneously signals your spinal cord to hold your body completely still. Science is still trying to determine exactly what physical function dreaming has for us, but since the 1950s, researchers have made remarkable advances in the study of sleep.

In centuries past, most people saw sleep as a kind of unconscious state or temporary death. The child's bedtime prayer may be a reference to the idea that the soul temporarily leaves the body: "Now I lay me down to sleep/I pray the Lord my soul to keep/If I should die before I wake/I pray the Lord my soul to take." But today we know that sleep is not merely a seven- or eight-hour period of total unconsciousness. You may be "dead to the world," but your mind is very much alive, cycling through periods of intense activity and periods of rest. The cycles of sleep are a fairly new discovery, but in the years since researchers finally cracked the code of sleep we have learned a great deal about what our bodies do when we dream. We now know that sleep is made of a pattern that alternates between a stage in which brain activity heightens and dreaming takes place and a stage of "quiet sleep," so called because you are generally sleeping without much disturbance, still and relaxed, without the rapid eye movement and accompanying brain waves that indicate dreaming.

You've probably heard of REM sleep, which is the particular stage of sleep we're in when we dream. The term *REM* stands for rapid eye movement, and this stage is so called because the eyes move back and forth beneath the eyelids, as though they are watching an action-packed movie. Watch someone sleeping sometime and you'll see how the eyelids seem to flutter as the eyes roll beneath them; if you are able to wake the person up during REM, chances are that he or she will be able to recall a dream, even if usually unable to do so after waking up in the morning. Awaken that person during non-REM, or quiet sleep, and he or she will be hard-pressed to recount any dream activity at all.

The discovery of rapid eye movement is legendary. In the early 1950s, in the University of Chicago laboratory of sleep researcher Nathaniel Kleitman, a graduate student named Eugene Asirinsky sat monitoring the staggering pen marks of an electroencephalograph (EEG) machine. The EEG machine's wires led to electrodes attached to an infant, whose brain waves were Asirinsky's focus of interest. The story goes that Asirinsky thought the machine was broken when the graph in front of him suddenly began to stagger wildly. After all, sleep was a period of rest. Only after checking the connecting wires did he discover the baby's rolling eyes. What could it mean?

Kleitman and Asirinsky, working together with medical student William C. Dement, began to research whether adults had these same eye movements during sleep. Awakening their research subjects during REM sleep led them to conclude in 1953 that REM sleep takes place only during the dream stage: Subjects roused during REM sleep were far better able to describe their dreams in vivid detail than those who slept through the night or were awakened during what came to be known as non-REM sleep. As Dement recalls in his book *Some Must Watch While Some Must Sleep,* "This was the break-through—the discovery that changed the course of sleep research from a relatively pedestrian inquiry into an intensely exciting endeavor pursued with great determination in laboratories and clinics all over the world."

The discovery of REM sleep led to other related conclusions about sleep and dreams. Whereas previous researchers had taken random EEG readings, Dement studied the entire night's sleep in several subjects over several days. This research allowed him to document regular periods of dreaming and sleeping. In this way, he was able to put to rest the notion that dreams occurred randomly as a result of indigestion, environmental noise, and other circumstances. Although scientists still couldn't say for sure why dreams occurred or where they came from, they were at least able to determine when they occurred and what things did not cause them.

THE SLEEP CYCLE

Thanks to these dream research pioneers, we now know that there is a regular cycle of sleeping and dreaming during each period of sleep. For most of us, a night of sleep begins with the usual rituals: checking to see if the front door is locked, turning out the lights, brushing the teeth, washing the face—whatever we have become accustomed to doing night after night. We change or remove our clothes. We get into bed, usually on the same side. Then it's lights out, and we lie in wait for the magic calm of sleep to overtake us.

Sleep then comes in an instant: One second you are awake, the next you are asleep. Here's what happens in the minutes preceding that fateful second in which you drop off. First, your body temperature drops. Your eyes close, and your brain waves begin regular alpha rhythms, indicating a relaxed state. Soon, Stage One sleep begins, as your muscles lose their tension, your breathing becomes more even, and your heart rate slows. A few minutes later, Stage Two sleep begins, and random or nonsensical images may float through your mind, mimicking the dream state. Occasionally, you may become alert enough to interrupt these hypnogogic dreams, or dreamlets. Resistance to falling asleep sometimes registers in these snippets—the myoclonic jerk, for example, that jolts you back to wakefulness, or the occasional involuntary movement or twitching you sometimes see in both humans and animals.

In time, you'll float on in to Stage Three sleep. Your body continues its slowdown process: Muscles lose all tightness, breaths come slowly and rhythmically, heart rate decreases, blood pressure falls. At this point, it would take a loud noise or other disturbance to pull you from your slumber. You are fully asleep.

Think of Stage Four sleep as deep sleep. If you do awaken from this type of sleep, you may well feel "fuzzy" or disoriented for a few minutes. Stage Four is considered to be the most physically restful period of sleep, and it is the longest in duration.

Where does dreaming fit in? Think of Stages One through Four as a cycle (see page 18). After about an hour and a half of moving through these stages, you cycle back through Stage One to resume Stage Two sleep, a lighter sleep in which your brain is more active. Indeed, brain waves show a great deal of activity. And here is where rapid eye movement begins. Surprisingly, studies show that it can be more difficult to awaken a sleeper during this lighter phase of sleep than any other. The body at this stage seems poised for "fight or flight." Remember how your heart and lungs seemed determined to put you into cold storage for the night? Your heart is slow and regular, your breathing deep and even. Then REM sleep takes you right out again. Your heart rate may fluctuate wildly, your breathing becomes irregular and fast. In fact, your breathing may become so shallow that, if you were awake, you would feel as if you were holding your breath, and might have to stop any second.

It is during this phase, which lasts from ten to sixty minutes

The Stages of Sleep

Stage One:
Non-REM Sleep
Your muscles relax, your pulse and breathing is slow, and your temperature drops slightly.

Stage Two:
Non-REM Sleep
Random images may float through your mind as the relaxation process continues.

REM!
Here, your rapid eye movement begins, your pulse quickens, your breathing becomes shallow, and you start to dream. This lasts from ten to sixty minutes.

Stage Three:
Non-REM Sleep
Muscles lose all tightness. Blood pressure falls. You are fully asleep.

Stage Two:
Non-REM Sleep
Prepare to dream. Brain activity increases.

Stage Four:
Non-REM Sleep
This is deep, dreamless sleep.

Stage Three:
Non-REM Sleep
You drift on toward lighter sleep.

each time, that dreams take place. Everyone has from five to seven dreams during a normal night's sleep, with each dream lasting from a few seconds to as much as an hour. These dreams do not occur in a flash; in fact, the perceived duration approximates the actual time spent dreaming. As each REM period ends, your body cycles back through Stages One through Four every ninety minutes until you awaken.

BODY DYNAMICS

The body goes through some interesting changes during the REM stage of the sleep cycle. Rapid eye movement is perhaps the most intriguing of these. Why do our eyes move back and forth as though we are watching a movie? Are we looking at imagined images? Yes and no. Studies show dreamers' eye movements do seem to coordinate with the action they see on their dream screens. Yet even those who have been blind from birth have rapid eye movement during Stage One sleep.

Despite the hyperactivity of the eyes, the body goes from a relaxed and almost motionless state during other stages of sleep to a fairly rigid position during REM sleep. Sure, hands and feet may jerk and twitch, and the face may register some expression or movement, but any instructions the brain might send to the muscles to move go straight to the dead-letter office, stuck in the spinal chord. Although a person generally moves during sleep, a *dreaming* person is incapable of moving during the REM period—at least voluntarily. (Contrary to popular belief, sleepwalking does not occur during the dream state.) Involuntary twitching or jerking may occur, however.

There are other physical characteristics of dreaming as well. In adults and infants alike, the head and chin relax so completely that researchers can use the slackening of the muscles under the chin as a reliable signal that REM sleep is occurring. This phe-

nomenon is not just restricted to humans: In rabbits, for example, the ears remain straight back on the head for all stages of
sleep. But when the rabbit starts to dream, the ears flop down on
either side. Other animals, such as dogs, cats, rats, and monkeys,
exhibit the same type of twitching, rapid breathing, and even
penile erections during their dreams. And REM sleep patterns have
been detected in every mammal investigated, as well as in birds.

A human male of any age (even infancy) will experience an
erection at the beginning of each REM period—even when his
dreams contain no sexual content whatsoever. These erections
occur about every eighty-five minutes, just before REM begins,
and last about twenty-five minutes. Does this timetable sound
familiar? It's roughly the same as the REM portion of the sleep
cycle. Why it happens is a mystery, but given that it happens
even when a dream has no sexual content, it may have to do
with the overall stimulation of the nervous system.

DREAM DEPRIVATION

It was Dement, by then a researcher at Mount Sinai Hospital in
New York, who first examined what happens when subjects are
prevented from dreaming. In 1960, Dement set up studies to
explore whether people who were allowed all stages of sleep
except for the REM period of dreaming would suffer any effects.
Sleeping in the laboratory, the subjects were awakened the
moment REM began to occur; a control group was awakened
several times a night during non-REM sleep. They were then
allowed to go back to sleep. This experiment went on for the
better part of a week, with the laboratory subjects sleeping
about six hours a night, without being permitted to dream.
During this time, most subjects became increasingly irritable,
exhibiting symptoms of anxiety and eating more than usual.
These symptoms were not apparent in the control group.

Interestingly, Dement and Fisher observed that the subjects tended to begin REM sleep more frequently on subsequent nights, as though to catch up on missed dream time. In a 1965 study, Dement found that one man, deprived of REM sleep for fifteen nights, exhibited marked personality changes that disappeared once he was allowed to dream again, which he did 120 percent more than usual. So there is something to making up for missed hours of sleep by sleeping in on a weekend or holi-

> *"EXISTENCE WOULD BE INTOLERABLE IF WE WERE NEVER TO DREAM."*
> *—Anatole France, French author*

day! People deprived of REM sleep for several days eventually exhibit rapid eye movement almost as soon as they fall asleep, foregoing the usual stages leading up to it. Does this evidence mean REM sleep is more important than non-REM sleep? Maybe so. Is the need psychological? Perhaps animals, too, try to make up REM sleep after deprivation periods. Is it physiological? Perhaps. Indeed, there are theorists in each camp, with the beliefs of countless others falling somewhere in between. Chapter 3 offers an overview of contemporary theories about why we dream and what our dreams mean. But first, let's examine what different cultures have believed about dreams over the centuries.

CHAPTER TWO

DREAMS THROUGH TIME
A HISTORY OF DREAMS IN VARIOUS CULTURES

Although interest in dreamwork continues to increase, there are still many people who downplay the significance of our nightly imaginings, dismissing dreams as the result of indigestion, unrest, or anxiety. But in other cultures, in other centuries, dreams were highly esteemed, and considered to be of primary significance. Throughout the world, dreams have been seen as an integral part of life, and their contents were akin to the sacred. Whether sent from a god, a demon, or an ancestor, or merely an expression of a wish or a fear, dreams were believed to contain a mystery worth deciphering.

What were these nocturnal adventures, and what might early humans have thought about them? We can only imagine. But one thing is clear: At least from the dawn of recorded history, people were compelled to interpret the meaning of the stories and images in their dreams. In fact, in centuries past, societies invested dreams with even more power and importance than the experiences of their waking lives. In ancient Greece and Rome, for example, dream interpreters actually accompanied military leaders into battle, so essential was the understanding of dream content. Over time, the Christian belief that dreams were the work of the devil influenced Western culture to such an extent that dream interpretation was discouraged, perhaps out of a fear that the content of dreams could undermine the moral teachings of the Church. But dream interpretation continues today, and while the focus has largely shifted from decoding a divine message sent by a deity to uncovering a meaning anchored in the dreamer's own psyche, the tendency to look for meaning remains, as it has for thousands and thousands of years, possibly from the beginning of time. Delving into the past to learn the history of dreamwork allows us to derive a cultural context for our own dream lives today. Just as tracing our family history builds stronger bonds with our relatives, tracing the history of dreamwork can enrich our lives as dreamers, making a connection with the past and forging a bond with our world community.

ANCIENT CULTURES

From the earliest days of written language, dreams and dream theories have been documented extensively. Sumerian texts, inscribed with sticks on clay tablets in 3000 to 4000 B.C., describe this Mesopotamian people's practices of dream interpretation, and indicate that dreams were believed to be messages from the gods. Dream reports in these now-fragmented texts seem to follow a particular format, experts report, that is not unlike the common guidelines for a dream journal today. Not only is the dream recounted, but background details about the dreamer are included as well, including where and when the dream took place, how the dreamer felt about the dream, and what message he or she derived from it.

In ancient Egypt, the dream interpreters were priests known as "masters of the secret things," who documented their findings in hieroglyphics, their picture alphabet. One such volume exists as part of an archeological discovery known as the Chester Beatty papyrus, an early dream interpretation book that is more than two thousand years old.

In many ancient cultures, priests and seers who had a talent for interpreting dreams were considered to be divinely gifted. A person who had a particularly significant dream was also believed to be blessed, and only certain people were considered worthy of such dreams. Artemidorus, author of the *Oneirocritica*, a five-volume book on the dream interpretation practiced by his Greco-Roman contemporaries, wrote in the second century A.D. that "Dreams are proportioned according to the party dreaming. Thus those of eminent persons will be great . . . if poor, their dreams will be very inconsiderable." (The *Oneirocritica* takes its name from Oneiros, a Greed dream messenger sent by the gods.)

In the *Oneirocritica,* Artemidorus refers to an already extensive body of literature on the subject of dreams. In the days of the Greek epic poet Homer (eighth century A.D.), "The dream was not conceived of as an internal experience, a state of mind, or a message from the irrational unconscious to the conscious ego," Susan Parman writes in *Dream and Culture.* "Rather, it was an objectified messenger, a supernatural agent sent by a deity (Zeus in *The Iliad*, Athena in the *Odyssey*), or in some cases by the dead." Later, she explains, ancient Greek authors such as Plato, Horace, Virgil, Statius, and Lucian embraced the concept of "true and false dreams," some prophetic, and some red herrings.

In ancient times, dreams were often—but not always—believed to be prophetic, and people of all cultures shared what they had dreamed in hopes of catching a glimpse of the future or receiving a message of advice or warning. The Egyptians, for instance, relied on an elaborately constructed list of interpretations, a kind of early dream dictionary. Author Raymond de Becker cites a few of these in his book *The Understanding of Dreams:* "If a woman kisses her husband, she will have trouble; if she gives birth to a cat, she will have many children; if she gives birth to an ass, she will have an idiot child." Even the ancient Greek philosopher Socrates considered dreams to be prophetic, emanating from the gods. For this reason, dreams figured prominently in ancient cultures' religious rituals intended to evoke the dream spirits or gods who would send these vivid messages.

In Buddhist culture, as in Taoism, Hinduism, and Sufism, the specifics of dreamwork were kept secret, considered to be sacred. In fact, there is a particular type of dream called *Milam Ter,* or "dream treasure," which, according to Michael Katz, editor of *Dream Yoga,* are "teachings that are considered to be the creations of enlightened beings. The training for dream awareness or lucidity, apparently thousands of years old, was purposefully hidden or stored in order to benefit future generations." Again, there was a decidedly prophetic overtone to this class of dreams.

The Old Testament written between about 750 and 100 B.C. according to the *Dictionary of the Bible,* makes numerous references to dreams, which the Hebrew people considered to be gifts from God, just like the waking visions that occur frequently in Scripture. The folk art toy called Jacob's Ladder is, in fact, named for an element in a dream recounted in the Bible: Jacob dreamed that a ladder connected earth to heaven, and that God stood at the top, instructing him and his family to spread God's word. Ancient Jews turned frequently to their dreams for such messages. Apart from a belief in dreams as gifts from God, there was also an element of belief in soul travel. The idea of recent waking experience and even the sleeping environment having an influence on dream content was another part of the framework. Remarkably, even these ancient people made a practice of expunging or changing dreams that were upsetting to them.

The Talmud, the collected commentary on biblical text that, along with the Old Testament, is part of the foundation of the Jewish religion, also mentions the use of dreams to predict the future, citing the potential of dreams to influence the decisions of kings and governments. Compiled between 200 B.C. and 300 A.D., the Talmud discusses the purpose of dreams extensively, purporting that dreams have meaning subject to interpretation and serving as a notable precursor to some contemporary theories. Its two thousand authors were primarily Phoenecian (Hebrew) and Babylonian, and it is assumed they were influenced greatly by the nearby cultures of Greece and Rome, which in turn would be influenced by the Talmud. There were two different schools of thought expressed in this document: that dreams come from higher powers, and that dreams are generated by the psyche, perhaps as opposing forces of the mind. Interestingly, the Talmud also contains references to dreams as wish fulfillment, which is how Sigmund Freud would later characterize all dream content.

The New Testament, written between 75 and 400 A.D., also includes countless references to dreams. And the interpretations have evolved over time. In Christianity's early days, for example, dreams were thought to be the work of God, designed to offer messages for both the dreamer and those to whom he reported the dream. Synesius of Cyrene, an early Christian bishop who wrote a book entitled *On Dreams,* found dreams to be of immeasurable inspiration and significance. Synesius saw dreams as a state in which the mind could work unfettered by the conventions dreamers adhered to in their waking lives, and therefore considered dreams to hold the power of transforming the dreamer by offering new insights and talents. This belief, dating to the writings of this fifth-century religious leader, evidences itself today in the current dreamwork movement.

Famous Biblical Dreams

The Old Testament and the New Testament both contain many references to dreams. Here, we summarize a few of the best-known biblical dreams.

Jacob's Ladder (Old Testament—Gen. 28: 10–16)

Jacob lay down on a pillow of rocks and fell asleep, dreaming he saw a ladder that led from Earth to Heaven, with "the angels of God ascending and descending on it." God stood at the top, announcing himself to Jacob, promising his blessing: "And behold I am with thee, and will keep thee in all places whither thou goest, and will bring thee again into this land: for I will not leave thee, until I have done that which I have spoken to thee of." (The child's folk art toy called "Jacob's Ladder" was inspired by this Bible story.)

Joseph's Dream (Old Testament—Gen. 37: 3–11)

An elderly man named Israel's youngest son Joseph, for whom he made a coat of many colors, was the object of much sibling rivalry. His brothers' jealousy grew when he reported his dream to them: "We were binding sheaves in the field, and lo, my sheaf arose, and also stood upright, and behold, your sheaves stood round about, and made obeisance to my sheaf." The brothers were enraged at the thought of Joseph reigning over them. When a second dream, in which the sun, moon, and stars, too, "made obeisance" to him, even Israel looked askance. (The twentieth-century musical *Joseph and the Amazing Technicolor Dreamcoat* was inspired by this Bible story.)

Joseph's Dream about the Birth of Christ (New Testament—Matt. 1: 18–21; 2: 12–14, 19–21; 27: 17–20)

When Mary's immaculate conception was first discovered, "an angel of the Lord appeared to [Joseph] in a dream, saying, 'Joseph, thou son of David, fear not to take unto thee Mary thy wife, for that which is conceived in her is of the Holy Ghost. And she shall bring forth a son, and thou shalt call his name Jesus: for he shall save his people from their sins.'" Other dreams followed, containing warnings from God himself, and the couple continued to heed them.

Still, dreams were in large part discounted as fanciful nonsense, perhaps because the nightly wanderings of an unchecked mind allowed for visions and experiences that sometimes went against religious dogma. In time, while some Western Christians continued to see dreams as divine gifts, others came to believe they were the work of demons. Perhaps most influential was the thirteenth-century priest St. Thomas Aquinas, whose writings remain influential today, particularly in the Catholic Church. Aquinas attempted to discount the possibility that dreams had special meaning, and attributed them to three different causes: waking experiences, physical sensations, and the work of God or demons. While he did not believe it was sinful to interpret the first two types of dreams, as earlier Christians had held, he did consider it "unlawful and superstitious" to derive meaning from dreams sent by demons.

The prophet Muhammad (570–632 A.D.), the Arabian founder of Islam to whom Moslems believe the Koran was dictated by God, considered dreams to have vital significance, and to have some bearing on the matters of waking life. He would inquire of his disciples every morning what their dreams were, discuss their interpretations, offer his own, and then recount his own dreams. According to Nathanial Bland, writing in *The New World of Dreams*, "By [one] dream attributed to him, the Sunnis justify the still-disputed rights of his three successors; and the origin of a strife, political and religious, which convulsed the whole Muhammaden empire and threatened its destruction, and which still divides the followers of Islam by a schismatic and irreconcilable hatred, is founded on a revelation made to its founder Muhammad in his sleep." Indeed, the dreams of the prophet had ramifications that reached beyond his own experiences to affect centuries of cultural conduct. It was during Muhammad's lifetime that dream interpretation was elevated to a science, called *Ibn ul Tabir*. Dream books, called *Tabir Namehs,* which commented on sleep and dreams, offered specific guidelines for their interpretation. Writes Bland: "*Tabir* is set forth as being a noble science, first taught by God himself to Adam, from Adam passing to Seth, and from Seth to Noah, by whom the Deluge was foretold in his explanation of dreams to Canaan's mother."

Ancient Arab dream practices prove to be a fascinating precursor to contemporary dreamwork. Their custom held that in order "to get a clear vision of what is happening or what will befall you in your life, you should do certain things before going to bed," writes Yehia Gouda, author of *Dreams and Their Meanings in the Old Arab Tradition*. Rituals such as this one for bedtime—which involves careful bodily cleansing, sleeping in a certain position, speaking a prayer or meditation, and fasting—are common in many cultures around the globe, and are quite similar to some modern dream practices described in chapter 6. Ancient Arabian dream interpreters, held in high esteem, followed certain rules in offering interpretations. According to Gouda, they believed the ideal time for recounting or interpreting a dream "is the early morning, when the dreamer's memory and the interpreter's mind are still fresh, before both of them get entangled in the worries and necessities of everyday life." Dream interpreters gave credit where they thought credit was due, to the dreamer him- or herself: "The best interpretation is that given by the dreamer himself, even if he knows nothing about the science or conventional symbols of dreams, for people have their own concepts and codes." And they acknowledged that dream symbolism could vary from one dreamer to the next: "The same dream experienced by two different persons could have two different meanings, depending on each person's nature and character," Gouda continues.

These ancient Arab ideas are strikingly similar to those expressed by contemporary Western dreamworkers and many psychotherapists. But they were in fact "the synthesis of at least four or five introductions I read in Arabic," Gouda explains. "The marvelous thing about the Arabs of ancient times is that they understood very well that dreams belonged to the realm of absolute freedom. To them nothing was taboo."

Indeed, since history's earliest days, dreams have influenced not only religious belief and conduct but the decisions of leaders

in politics and battle, the choices of individuals in personal crisis, and the actions of medical professionals in treating illness. It
is common in our culture for people to experience healing
dreams, which contain some kind of message that speaks to the
health concerns of the dreamer: A dream of loose teeth, for
instance, might lead to a necessary trip to the dentist. In some
ancient cultures, dreams were considered a vital clue to the
health of the dreamer. In ancient Greece, for example, physicians
used the information contained in dreams to make a diagnosis.
Sometimes, a doctor would turn to his own dreams for help in
treating a patient. For example, Galen, a well-known surgeon of
second-century Greece, would seek instruction from his dreams,
relying almost solely on this guidance to perform operations.
People would visit temples and other holy places for the specific
purpose of having a dream experience that could aid in healing
them. Aesclepius, a skilled physician living in eleventh-century
Greece came to be regarded as a god for his power as a healer.
He was often represented by a snake, so dreamers would sometimes seek out a place to sleep and dream where snakes were
known to live. Aesclepius would listen to the words of his
dreaming patients in order to devise a cure. And legend has it
that even after his death there were hundreds of sleeping temples
dedicated to him where the ill and infirm could go to dream their
own cures.

In many ancient cultures, dream life and waking life were
simply two different dimensions of a single existence, a view-
point that shows itself in many modern cultures and that is
shared by many contemporary dream theorists as well. For the
ancient Egyptians, the world of dreams was indeed an actual
place they visited when their souls left their bodies to travel
freely during sleep. The Talmud, too, refers to these soul travels,
but suggests that the world the soul visits is not a different world
from the one the dreamer inhabits in waking life.

Another ancient topic of dreams is sexual content, which received notice in all cultures long before Sigmund Freud's theories of sexuality gained prominence. In numerous cultures, a sexual dream indicated visitation from a sexual demon, the *incubus* and *secubus* of Greek legend. Like the mythical Greek faun, the Talmud's erotic demon is hairy and goatlike. Lilith is another erotic demon of Talmudic origin: Taking on either a masculine or feminine form, she attacks only people sleeping alone in a house. This character is essentially the same as *incubus/secubus*, perhaps not surprising given the influence of Greco-Roman belief on the writings of this ancient document.

In ancient China, writes psychologist Robert Van de Castle in *Our Dreaming Mind,* dreams were believed to be "nighttime excursions to the land of the dead," embarked upon by the soul, or *p'o*, which could separate from the body during sleep in order to make these visits. Almost a thousand years ago, a Chinese mathematician wrote a document entitled *Chou Kung's Book of Auspicious and Inauspicious Dreams,* which categorizes dreams and offers interpretations that today sound rather like fortune cookie pronouncements. If you dream that you witness the flight of a swallow, for instance, "a friend will come to visit you from far away." Dream rituals pervaded ancient Chinese culture. Like the people of ancient Greece, the Chinese would habitually visit temples, sleep on graves, or perform rituals so as to incubate their dreams, looking for answers that might lead them to a course of action. Indeed, dreams were held in such high esteem that political officials routinely sought guidance from their dreams, which they then shared with their colleagues. Interestingly, Van de Castle also points out, this culture's ancient beliefs about the dream state still resonate today: Because the ancient Chinese believed a soul could fail to return to the body if the dreamer were suddenly awakened, some Chinese people today are quite wary of alarm clocks.

In ancient India, as in so many other ancient cultures, dreams have received much attention in sacred writings over the centuries. As always, people were inclined to translate dreams, identifying certain dream symbols as omens of good or bad things to come. Curiously, the Vedas, the sacred books of ancient India that were written as long ago as 1500 B.C., contain references to different periods of

> "I AM INDEED A PRACTICAL DREAMER. . . .
> I WANT TO CONVERT MY DREAMS INTO
> REALITIES AS FAR AS POSSIBLE."
> —Mahandas Gandhi, Indian statesman

sleep which Western researchers did not identify scientifically until the mid-twentieth century! Briefly, these periods of sleep were established as a measure for how soon after the dream its prophecy would come true. Indian dream texts also suggest that a dreamer who remembers several dreams upon waking should interpret only the final dream. This belief is remarkably like that of modern dream interpreters, who refer to the dream remembered upon awakening as most likely the last dream dreamed and the one most closely connected with waking experience.

CONTEMPORARY NONWESTERN CULTURES

Dreams continue to be held in high esteem in cultures outside Western culture. There are still dreamers throughout the world who accept their dreams' gifts, heed their dreams' warnings, and seek out their dreams' adventures as a regular part of their cultural life. In many cultures today, among them New Guinea's Arapesh, Mexico's Tarahumara, and several Native American tribes, dreams serve as an alternate dimension to waking life, with knowledge to be gained from the experiences that unfold each night. Like some ancient cultures, Australia's Aborigines, the continent's native hunters and gatherers, today maintain their belief that the dreamworld is an actual place, a spiritual dimension they call "Dreamtime"; it is here that they look to connect with their ancestors, whom they call "Dreamings." These ancestral beings are considered to be more powerful than living people and to have nonhuman manifestations such as rocks or trees. Rather than creating the dreams, like a god or demon would, these ancestors merely live in dreams, and it is to dreams that the living must travel in order to make contact. One way in which this contact is useful is in the creation of art: Songs, stories, and artwork inspired by dreams are considered to be the gifts of the ancestors, channeled through the dreamer, who is merely the vehicle of reproduction for the ancestor's original creation. These traditions continue among the Aborigines today, echoing the ancient practice in many cultures of creating song, dance, painting, sculpture, and household objects based on dream content.

Other twentieth-century cultures, too, have chosen to incorporate dreams into their daily life as a matter of course, often with remarkable results. In the 1930s, archaeologist Kilton Stewart traveled deep into the mountains of what is now Malaysia to study the Senoi, a minority tribe of 12,000 people who he said appeared at that time to live in extraordinary harmony, with very little fighting, stealing, anger, upset, or mental illness. In search of an explanation, Stewart came to regard their intense dreamwork activity as the reason for their peaceful existence. Although it is unclear how many of the Senoi people participate in these dream practices, his reports are still fascinating and useful for dreamers today.

According to Stewart, the Senoi believed the dreamworld to be just as real as the waking world, however different. They believed the conflicts they experienced in waking life found expression in their dreams. By talking about these dreams,

Stewart suggested, the conflicts were put to rest, rather than causing the dreamer to take some physical action that could result in strife. Unlike most Westerners, who are at times embarrassed by their dream content, the Senoi saw nothing wrong with dreams, instead viewing even incestuous dreams as merely "facets of one's own spiritual or psychic makeup." Interestingly, the beliefs of these isolated Malaysian forest dwellers are strikingly similar to some contemporary dream theories put forward by Western dreamworkers, especially the idea that every person, place, and thing in a dream is in fact representative of a part of the dreamer.

From childhood, Stewart reported, Senoi children learned to participate actively in their dreams, confronting danger, interacting with even the most sinister dream characters, and gathering "gifts" of insight and information that they can bring back with them to their waking world. Being aware of a dream while in the dream (an experience called lucid dreaming) enables the dreamer to make decisions and take actions that influence the dream's outcome and, therefore, its usefulness in waking life. It is a rarer skill among Western dreamers, but Stewart reported that Senoi children were encouraged to perfect it from the time they could first recount their dreams. Each morning, the Senoi gathered for dream sharing, looking to the content of the tribe's dreams for all kinds of information, from where to hunt that day to what songs and dances to add to their rituals.

Interestingly, Stewart's findings were later disputed. Although Senoi dreamwork was found to occur, Stewart apparently exaggerated the extent of it, as well as the Senoi's resulting peacefulness. There were in fact occasional incidences of discord, violence, and mental illness in Senoi life. (One anthropologist, who went to live among the Senoi in the 1930s, learned this the hard way: When H. D. "Pat" Noone forbade his Senoi wife to sleep with Noone's adopted Senoi brother, the brother shot him to death with a blowpipe.) Sociologist G. William Domhoff sought to determine the truth about Stewart's much-disputed claims in his 1985 book *The Mystique of Dreams: A Search for Utopia through Senoi Dream Theory*. Domhoff concludes that Kilton Stewart's "preoccupation [with] the major social problems that faced the civilized world" led him to ascribe to Senoi dream traditions a kind of healing power that could solve the problems of violence and mental illness. "His desire to be a great healer and prophet led him to imbue his dream principles with the mystique of the nonviolent and easygoing Senoi," writes Domhoff. "It was Kilton Stewart who developed the novel idea that societies can benefit from sharing their dreams and that they can shape them through . . . mind control."

Exposure to dominant peoples and the amenities of modern life has irrevocably changed the Senoi way of life. Nonetheless, Kilton Stewart's theories are worth noting, if only because Senoi dream theory has enjoyed popularity among Western dream-workers and dream researchers for several generations. Times have changed, even for the Senoi, and their once idyllic life has lost its innocence as the twentieth century has invaded their culture. Yet while some of Stewart's claims have been questioned, it is still interesting to consider the effect regular dreamwork can have on individuals and an entire culture.

On the African continent, there are many variations in the way different tribal peoples view dreams and dreamwork. Some look to dreams for their healing power, others might look for divine messages, and still others rely on dreams to guide their artistic creation. Among Zezuru healers in Zimbabwe, for example, dreams are said to be the source of all training on the medicinal use of plants, and also serve as a diagnostic tool, according to the University of Zimbabwe's Pamela Reynolds, who worked with sixty traditional healers of the region. And for all Zezuru people, dreams hold special interpretive possibilities that can shape waking experience. She writes, "Zulu believe that without dreams, true and uninterrupted living is not possible. Zezuru believe the same: dreamless nights are said to be unhealthy."

The Temne of Sierra Leone, too, look to dreams for divine training. "Among the Temne, the vision and knowledge of diviners are largely attributed to accomplishment in dreaming, through which they become experts on the dreams of their clients. Not only, then, do their dreams have power; they have power over other people's dreams," writes Rosalind Shaw, co-editor of *Dreaming, Religion, and Society in Africa*. This same volume includes an essay by Roy M. Dilley of the University of St. Andrews about the Tukolor, who believe dreams are associated with spiritual agents, and that in dreams the soul is allowed to roam free. To the Tukolor, some dreams are utter nonsense, others are meaningless entertainment, and still others are incubated to reveal new techniques they can use in their traditional weavings. Africa is a massive continent, and it is not surprising that dream beliefs vary from culture to culture. And, contrary to the stereotypes that are associated with native peoples, not all African tribes invest dreams with special significance. The Berti, for instance, "are not encouraged to dream and to remember their dreams," according to Ladislav Holy, also of the University of St. Andrews. In fact, they rarely tell their dreams to others, and claim not to dream very often at all, despite the biological evidence Western researchers have gathered showing that all people (and mammals) dream every night.

Like many societies on the African continent, the Native American tribes of North America have traditionally looked to dreams for healing, which they believe is often symbolized by the appearance of an animal or bird. Despite vastly diverse cultures among the few thousand Native American tribes who populated this continent when the Europeans first landed, every tribe placed a great deal of importance on dream life. Contacting supernatural spirits and borrowing from their power was common in all of these cultures. A dream interpreter, like a medicine man, had special status in the tribe, and was consulted regularly. Rituals designed to filter bad dreams and attract good ones incorporated the use of a dream catcher, a small, handcrafted net that is decorated with symbolic objects such as feathers and beads.

The seventeenth- and eighteenth-century Iroquois tribe held that dreams shed light on human nature and could also provide insight and guidance, according to Susan Parman, author of *Dream and Culture*. Parman writes: "The Iroquois took their dreams very seriously, and interpreted them as the wishes of supernatural beings, or as enactments of personal fate they were destined to fulfill." The dream as destiny is a theme that surfaces in other Native American cultures as well.

In tribes such as the Sioux, dreams were a rite of passage for adolescents on the path to adulthood. Dreams were considered tools for guidance, and it was with this aim that a teenage Sioux would embark alone on a vision quest, in search of a sign from a guardian spirit as to what life plan to make. "Unarmed and naked, except for loincloth and moccasins, he would go out into the prairie, exposing himself to sun, danger, and hunger, and tell the deity of his essential humility and need of guidance," social psychologist Erik Erikson wrote in *Childhood and Society*. After several days, a dream, or sometimes a waking vision, would appear and the child would return home to face a team of dream experts who would interpret the vision and tell him of his future: hunter, warrior, medicine man, conjurer, priest, artist, or even dream interpreter—whatever role seemed to be indicated. Upon the child's return, members of the tribe would create a personal ceremonial shield based on the results.

Once an essential part of life, the practice of the vision quest is no longer popular among Native Americans, as traditions have receded into memory. But many of the traditional songs and dances preserved as part of the Native American heritage contain vestiges of the vision quest, and the artifacts created today—pottery, jewelry, blankets, paintings, drums, pipes, head-dresses, shields—are decorated with what began as dream images. Many modern dreamers use Native American cus-toms—sweat baths, fasting, chanting, meditation, and other purification rituals—to conduct their own vision quests or dream incubations. (Later chapters incorporate some of these techniques into modern dreamwork exercises.)

A belief in the dream as prophecy shows up all over the world, in all different eras. Not only in Native American culture, where a single dream experience was seen to determine a boy's future, but in many eras, in many countries. Buddhist legend has it that before the birth of the Buddha, his mother, Queen Maya, dreamed of a sacred white elephant entering her body, a sign that she was carrying a great leader. Ancient Egyptian dream books foretold fortunes based on the contents of dreams. And throughout the Bible, dreams are used as prophecy.

EARLY WESTERN BELIEFS

Whereas some cultures embraced dream life as an important dimension, worthy of interpretation and exploration, Western Christian culture emphasized only the most literal or transpar-ently symbolic interpretations, so threatened was that culture by the possibility that dream content might undermine the morality being handed down by the Church. Despite numerous biblical references to dream interpretation, the practice was discouraged as frivolous, if not dangerous, perhaps partly influenced by the early Christian belief that dreams were sent by the devil. Philosopher Jeremy Taylor, writing in 1650, warned readers to pay dreams no mind: "If you suffer impressions to be made upon you by dreams, the devil hath the reins in his own hands, and can tempt you by that, which will abuse you, when you can make no resistance."

By the middle of the next century, there is some discussion of whether all dreams are the work of the devil. Essayist Daniel Dafoe, writing in 1750, observed that "trifling dreams are the product of the mind being engaged in trifling matters; a child dreams of its play, a housewife dreams of her kitchen . . . ; these have nothing of apparition in them; nothing of angels or spirits, God or devil, but when dream comes up to vision, and the soul is embarked in a superior degree, then you may conclude you have had some extraordinary visitors." If those "visitors" encouraged the dreamer to do good, then they were godly; if they encouraged the dreamer to do evil, then they were demonic.

Even as people were writing about the spiritual influences of dreams and their interpretive possibilities, there were theorists determined to persuade the world that dreams were the results of purely physical functioning, the natural by-product of a sleeping organ. After all, argued philosopher Thomas Hobbes in 1650, our hearts continue to beat, our lungs to breathe, why not our brain to think, even though it is sleeping? As to whether these mental wanderings had any meaning, there were as many questions as possible answers. Hobbes and others held that physical sensations during sleep gave rise to certain types of dreams—feeling cold caused a scary dream, feeling warm caused an angry dream, and so forth.

By the mid-nineteenth century, the belief in a divine source of dreams definitely had begun to ebb, and theories such as

Hobbes' became more widely accepted. French psychologist Alfred Maury, for example, made an exhaustive study of dreams, concluding that they resulted from the misinterpretation of sense impressions during sleep: A loud noise during the night, for instance, could cause a dream about a thunderstorm. Indeed, some dreams are influenced by surrounding experiences. (Have you ever awakened to a clock radio only to discover the songs and commentary had been incorporated into your dreamlets just before you woke up? Or heard a loud rushing sound in a dream that turned out to be an air-conditioning or heating vent?). But modern research shows that people also dream regularly in rooms in which there is absolutely no environmental stimulation. Still, Maury's commitment to scientific dream experimentation is significant, serving as a precursor of the intensive—and productive—research that would follow in the century to come.

As progress continued into the early twentieth century, other, more sophisticated physiological theories began to arise. The dreams people experienced while falling asleep, went the theory of nineteenth-century scientist George Trumbull Ladd, were caused by "excitement of the retina by intra-organic stimulation." (In this, he may have loosely predicted REM sleep, which, as chapter 5 discusses, is part of the basis for a contemporary neurologically based explanation for dreaming.) In the morning, Ladd reasoned, it was the external stimulation of sunlight that caused dreams. Ladd characterized a night of sleep as "a series of naps interrupted by more or less partial awakening"—again predicting the eventual discovery of cycles of sleep not confirmed until 1953, half a century after the 1892 publication of his theories.

An examination of the literary history of the world reveals that a dream interpretation dictionary was among the first "best-sellers" in the Western world. With the invention of the printing press in 1622, books were within the grasp of a far greater public than ever before. Naturally, the Bible was the most popular book printed. Second only to the Bible was a book called *Oneirocritics,* which psychologist Calvin Hall calls "the Adam of all dream books." There were others before that, among them the Sumerian, Egyptian, and Muhammaden texts. And hundreds, perhaps thousands, of others have followed, as people have continued to seek understanding of their dreams.

One such book, published around the time of Sigmund Freud's *The Interpretation of Dreams,* is *Ten Thousand Dreams Interpreted, or What's in a Dream,* by Gustavus Hindman Miller (reissued in 1992 by Smithmark Publishers under the title *A Dictionary of Dreams: An Alphabetical Journey Through the Images of Sleep*). This volume, first released in 1909, holds that dreams tell our fortunes, and we have only to understand what their various symbols mean to know our futures. The book today seems whimsical and charming, reflecting as it does a very different culture from the one we know today. Entries are at times obscure, and to contemporary culture seem arbitrary, though one can imagine the book was received with great seriousness in its day as the definitive answer to the cryptic puzzle dreams presented. The entries are very specific, and include such items as "Hemp seed: To see hemp seed in dreams denotes the near approach of a deep and continued friendship. To the business man, is shown favorable opportunity for money-making." Another favorite lists "Embroidery: If a woman dreams of embroidering, she will be admired for her tact and ability to make the best of everything that comes her way. For a married man to see embroidery, signifies a new member in his household; for a lover, this denotes a wise and economical wife."

Notable here are the predictive qualities of each entry—the dream elements predict what will happen in the dreamer's life—

and also the obscurity of the images, which, though not unheard of, are not a common part of American culture today. Miller, in the preface to this dictionary, has this to say about the psychic power of dreams: "To dream at night and the following day have the thing dreamed of actually take place, or come before your notice, is . . . the higher or spiritual sense living or grasping the immediate future ahead of the physical mind." Miller's book was published at the end of an era in which Western culture believed dreams to be mystical and prophetic. With the dawn of Freudian theory, and the many schools of thought that have followed, a new era began, an era in which psychology and science have united in search of the truth about dreams.

TOWARD A TWENTIETH-CENTURY PICTURE

It is interesting to note that many ancient cultural beliefs have found their way into contemporary theories. Certainly, the commitment to interpretation as a means of gaining insight and understanding remains strong among dreamworkers. But consider that the Old Arab practices of bedtime rituals and crediting the dreamer with the creation of the dream differ very little from the contemporary dreamwork techniques that have been developed in the last fifty years. Consider also that the Talmudic premise that dreams express wish fulfillment is echoed in Sigmund Freud's pioneering theory of the dream as an expression of repressed sexual and aggressive urges. (Freud had a long-standing interest in African tribal beliefs, some of which hold to the idea of dreams as wish fulfillment.) That the people of India divided sleep into different periods throughout the night is at least a coincidental precursor of the scientifically proven cycles of REM and non-REM sleep. That a nineteenth-century scientist might make the connection between visual stimulation and dreams seems part of a path toward fuller knowledge of the process of dreaming.

Despite much evidence, then as now, about the healing, spiritual, and even prophetic power of dreams, there is still a current school of thought that considers dream content to be the random result of neurons in the brain continuing to fire in the absence of waking experience. This stance is very familiar, with considerable evidence to support it, yet it seems to echo past arguments that dreams are merely the result of physical discomfort or indigestion. Indeed, the dream theories of today have their basis in thousands of years of belief and experience. The next chapter traces contemporary dream theory from its roots to its many branches.

CHAPTER THREE

MODERN DREAM THEORISTS
WHO SAYS
WHAT
ABOUT DREAMS

Contemporary dream theorists generally see things quite differently than people of previous centuries, though there are some striking echoes of the past. What mainstream dream theorists have abandoned is the ancients' belief that dreams are divinely inspired messages sent by gods to foretell the future or by demons to deceive the dreamer. No longer do they think that dreams bear no relation to the dreamer's own thoughts and experiences. And gone from the writings of modern dream theorists is the idea that dream content might undermine Christian standards of moral conduct.

Primitive societies of many origins tended to consider the content of dreams to be more significant than their waking lives—not surprising since they believed dreams to be messages from a deity. Are dream experiences *more* important than waking ones? Perhaps not. But there is some holdover from this ancient outlook: Although dreams may not be more important than waking life, most modern dream theorists argue, they *can* offer significant insight into character and conflict that our waking thoughts might miss.

As recently as the 1800s, scientists considered dreams meaningless, and blamed them on indigestion or physical discomfort such as excessive heat or cold. It is only in this century that dreams have been the focus of in-depth scientific study, with recordable data that show not only when we dream, but how and why we dream and what we dream about. And while theories still differ, and some scientists are even returning to a physiological explanation of dreams, there is new understanding that benefits all dreamers. Here is a summary of the history of twentieth-century dream theory.

SIGMUND FREUD

We've all heard references to the work of Sigmund Freud (1859–1939), the founder of psychoanalysis (the theory and therapeutic treatment of neuroses) and the first physician to see dreams as a "window to the soul." Before Freud, there had been considerable philosophical interest in dreams, but it was he who began to turn it into a science. Freud started his medical career as a neurologist, and initially sought to discover neurological causes of dreams. Finding no evidence to support this hypothesis, he turned toward psychology, studying hypnosis, which aroused his interest in looking at mental illness from a psychological rather than a physiological point of view. In time, he created a system for the individual interpretation of dreams that would change the course of dreamwork forever. As the first contemporary theorist to reexamine dreams as a wholly psychic (mental) process, Freud was a pioneer, bringing the study of dreams into the modern scientific world.

Freud not only used the study of dreams in his work with his patients, but also in conducting his own self-analysis. Examining his dreams led Freud to deduce that his dreams revealed he was actually happy about the death of his father, biographers say, which motivated him to explore dreams as expressions of emotions typically held back in waking life. Freud published the results of his work with the dreams of psychiatric patients in twenty-six different volumes, including *The Interpretation of Dreams* (1900), which he liked to call his "dream book." Although it initially aroused little interest, selling only 351 copies in the first six years, Freud himself considered it to be his "most significant work"; in the preface to its third edition in 1931, he called it "the most valuable of all the discoveries it has been my good fortune to make. Insight such as this falls to one's lot but once in a lifetime."

This landmark book chronicles his use of free association—saying whatever comes to mind—as a technique for understanding how the content of dreams is connected with a patient's waking life; Freud's technique of noting all of the dreamer's associations with a dream or dream symbol is still popular in dream interpretation today. Freud believed dreams came from the unconscious, that part of the brain that represses (holds back) or forgets memories, though even these supposedly lost emotions can usually be recalled. (Some people refer to it as the subconscious, though unconscious is the preferred term.) In trying to imagine the unconscious, it may help to think of your brain as an office building: The front room is your waking experience; the back room is your memory, easily accessible, logically filed; and the storage area beyond the back room is your unconscious, hard to get to sometimes, and elaborately cross-referenced with everything you have experienced in some surprising ways.

What is the purpose of dreams? As Freud saw it, dreams express buried sexual and aggressive impulses or wishes that are not safe or appropriate to reveal in everyday life; the unconscious takes over during sleep, he theorized, and it is from there that dreams emerge, providing a kind of mental release valve for these strong feelings.

Freud described two different levels of dream elements: the manifest dream content, the dream's basic story line as the dreamer recalls it; and the latent dream content, the unconscious wishes the dreamer has suppressed. Freud believed the latent dream content is where the true meaning lies. If you are wondering why the meaning of dreams is sometimes so hard to figure out, Freud would say it's because your conscious mind cannot deal with the latent dream content up front, so your unconscious steps in to shield or conceal the meaning from you by disguising the sexual or aggressive longings.

Freud suggested that the mind masks these often "inappropriate" desires by substituting a symbol for the unexpressed wish. In this way, the latent dream content is depicted through the symbolic manifest dream content. Freud was preoccupied with sexual content in dreams because he believed that dreaming is largely about the sexual urges repressed in early childhood; it is for this reason that any elongated object is considered a phallic or penislike symbol, and any cavity or container-type object a symbol of the vagina in Freudian interpretation. Dream activity such as flying or floating also bears some relation to a repressed sexual wish, according to Freud.

So, when people say "Oh, that's so Freudian," they are generally referring to an action or statement that appears to have an unconscious motivation—usually sexual or aggressive. A Freudian interpretation of a dream, then, would be scrutinized for these impulses: If you dream you cannot move, Freudian theory would suggest, you are holding back sexual feelings; if you dream you are falling, you are contemplating giving in to a sexual urge, and so forth. Freud considered these kinds of symbols and themes to be so typical and pervasive as to be virtually universal, meaning essentially the same thing to every dreamer. He still insisted, however, that every dream has some connection to an event in the dreamer's own personal history. Freud concluded that dreams are a direct route to understanding an individual's unconscious motivations, calling dreams "the royal road to a knowledge of the unconscious activities of the mind."

It is interesting to consider that Freud began his dream research at the end of the Victorian era, which is known for its intense sexual repression. The normal sexual and aggressive urges had to go somewhere, it seems, and the unconscious seemed to Freud to be the logical place. But these views made Freud one of the most unpopular and criticized members of the scientific community in Germany at the time. Against enormous opposition, however, Freud persisted in emphasizing the importance of sexuality in dreams and psychological development. In his preface to the second edition of *The Interpretation of Dreams* (1909), Freud expressed frustration that his fellow psychiatrists were resistant to his views: "My colleagues seem to have taken no trouble to overcome the initial bewilderment created by my new approach to dreams," he wrote. "The professional philosophers . . . have evidently failed to notice that we have something here from which a number of inferences can be drawn that are bound to transform our psychological theories."

In 1902, together with psychiatrists Alfred Adler, William Stekel, Carl Jung, among others, Freud established the Wednesday Psychological Group, a regular gathering of professionals that in time became the Vienna Psycho-Analytical Society. Little more than a decade later, Stekel, Adler, and Jung ended their affiliation with Freud. These early dream theorists developed their own theories, which differed from Freud's beliefs about the individual unconscious.

Sigmund Freud

The father of modern psychiatry, Sigmund Freud was born May 6, 1856, in what was formerly Czechoslovakia, the first of eight children born to Jewish wool merchant Jakob Freud and his wife, the former Amalie Nathanson.

When he was six, his family moved to Vienna, Austria, where he would grow up and attend medical school, entering the University of Vienna in 1873. His interest in science led him to study histology and neurophysiology.

Freud was among the first to examine the effects of cocaine on the nervous system, finding it to be an effective anesthetic. It was study at a Paris asylum that inspired his interest in the workings of the human mind.

As a neuropathologist, he continued to explore the workings of the physical brain, trying to determine the extent to which neuroses were chemically based.

Freud created the term *psychoanalysis* to describe the revolutionary free association technique he had developed to help disturbed patients reveal and confront repressed memories of emotional trauma. His focus on repressed sexual and aggressive urges as the primary content of dreams and the cause of neurosis made him an extraordinarily controversial figure in early post-Victorian Europe.

Still, through organizations such as the Wednesday Psychological Group, the Vienna Psycho-Analytical Society, and others, he influenced a generation of psychiatric professionals whose work is the basis for contemporary mental health theory and practice.

In addition to his landmark book *The Interpretation of Dreams* (1900), Freud is the author of numerous works, among them *Beyond the Pleasure Principle* (1920), *The Analysis of the Ego* (1920), *The Ego and the Id* (1923), *Inhibitions, Symptoms, and Anxiety* (1923), his *Autobiography* (1926), and *Civilization and Its Discontents* (1929).

Freud died of cancer in 1939.

CARL JUNG

Carl Jung (1875–1961), one of the most renowned dream theorists of modern times, worked with Freud for several years before the two scientists had a dispute over the existence of a "disguise function" in dreams that supposedly suppresses sexual and aggressive wishes; they also disagreed on how much influence sexual conflict really has in dreams. Jung considered the "disguise" theory to be too contrived, believing "the dream is a natural event and there is no reason under the sun why we should assume that it is a crafty device to lead us astray." In order to discover the meaning of dreams, Jung focused on what the manifest content of the dream might reveal, rather than what it seemed to *conceal*. He disagreed with Freud as to whether the meaning was *necessarily* connected to the dreamer's sexuality or wish fulfillment. Though he did not deny that sexual or aggressive wishes could surface in dreams, he did not believe that they are always present. Rather, a dream might have any number of meanings, finding references in the conscious and unconscious, personal and universal.

In this regard, Jung reached back into earlier cultural interpretations of dreams, arguing that some of a dream's content is based on experiences beyond those of the individual dreamer. He theorized that, in addition to a personal unconscious belonging to each individual dreamer, there is a collective unconscious shared by all humankind, complete with images and symbols that have had similar meaning in all cultures for centuries. In this regard, suggests author Raymond de Becker, Jung may have been influenced by the German philosopher Friedrich Nietzsche, who "placed the cause of dreams in the remote past of the human species, asserting that in our sleep we reenact the labours of early man." In metaphorical terms, let's extend our idea of the office suite with the front room (conscious mind), back room (memory), and storage area (unconscious): The collective unconscious could be seen as the building that contains all of the office suites that are the basic aspects of humanity, familiar and constant, no matter who moves in or out over generations.

Jung referred to "the contents of the collective unconscious" as archetypes. Although the term or idea of an archetype had occurred in earlier religious and mythological discussions, Jung was the first to identify the psychological archetype. Calling these universal symbols "among the inalienable assets of every psyche," Jung used archetypes to refer to the universal aspects of humankind that can have both "a positive favourable meaning or a negative evil meaning." You can think of archetypes as the essential "programming"—part of the original package that comes with your psychological computer. Archetypal symbols surface in dreams, which Jung called "the spontaneous products of the unconscious psyche . . . not falsified by any conscious purpose." In other words, your dreaming mind is free to make any symbolic reference, without the limitations the conscious mind might place on thought or imagination.

Generally, certain archetypes are capitalized in written form to emphasize their fundamental truth, thus an archetypal

Mother is, in effect, the Mother of us all. Sometimes, an archetype is given a Latin or Greek name as an indication of its mythic quality. For example, Jung identified *anima* and *animus* as the feminine and masculine parts of the opposite sex, the *anima* being a man's feminine side, and the *animus* being a woman's masculine side. Jung believed it was important to look at those opposite sex parts of the self in order for the self to be integrated or in balance. Working with dream images of members of the opposite sex is one way to come to terms with the masculine and feminine parts of ourselves and others.

Another powerful archetypal image is the Shadow Figure, who represents the darker side of the self. This shadow character is generally the same sex as the dreamer, and may take the form of a thief, a murderer, or any threatening figure. According to Jung, this negative aspect of the self exists in every human being in some form or another; dreams are one way to achieve the necessary expression and acknowledgment of this dark side. Other archetypes of special significance in Jungian dream theory include Water, the Pyramid, and the Circle.

Jung believed that the dreamer could converse or "dialogue" with these aspects of the dream to discover hidden messages. This was the beginning of taking dream analysis outside the psychiatrist's office and into the dreamer's hands. Unfortunately, the complexity of the archetypal references Jung used made it difficult for the dreamer to work without professional guidance. It remained for other theorists, working in the second half of this century, to develop new methods of interpretation. Not all dream theorists today would agree with Jung that there is necessarily one big memory out there connecting us all, but they do remain interested in the research he did to further the knowledge of dream symbols and what they represent.

CARL GUSTAV JUNG

Carl Gustav Jung was born in 1875 to a Swiss family with a long line of clergymen on both sides. However, Jung broke with this strong family tradition and decided to become a psychiatrist. He may have been influenced in this choice by his mother and maternal grandmother who were purported to have psychic abilities. Jung joined the staff of the Burghölzi Asylum of the University of Zurich in 1900, working with Eugen Bleuler on groundbreaking research into mental illness, including the delineation of the term *complex* to explain a patient's peculiar response to various words caused by his or her repressed associations.

Shortly thereafter, Jung began an intensive relationship with Sigmund Freud and for a period of five years (1907-1912) was his closest collaborator. They had several disagreements, however, both personal and professional, culminating in Jung's publication of *The Psychology of the Unconscious,* which challenged many of Freud's ideas about sexuality and the unconscious. The two men also disagreed about the existence of psychic phenomena, in which Jung strongly believed in and which Freud doubted. Though Jung had been elected president of the International Psychoanalytic Society and was considered to be Freud's successor, he ended his correspondence with Freud in 1913, breaking off from him in perhaps the same way he did from his own father, and resigned from the society in 1914. In his last letters to Freud, Jung complained about what he felt was Freud's patronizing and paternalistic attitude.

Jung went on to found his own brand of analytic psychology, based upon his interest in myths, legends, dreams, and symbols. He also developed the psychological distinction of two classes of people—extroverted and introverted—and later described four functions of the mind—thinking, feeling, sensations, and intuition. These distinctions are widely used today in many contemporary psychological techniques.

Jung wrote throughout his life on a variety of topics, including dreams, literature, and religion. Many of these writings appear in the twenty-volume *Collected Words of C.G. Jung* (1966 2nd ed.) and in *Modern Man in Search of a Soul* (1933). Also illuminating are his autobiographical book *Memories, Dreams, Reflections* (1962) and *Man and His Symbols* (1968), which was written for the general reader by Jung and his associates just before his death.

Jung lived until the age of eighty-five in Zurich with his wife, Emma, who contributed greatly to his work.

OTHER PSYCHOANALYTIC OR NEO-FREUDIAN THEORIES OF DREAM INTERPRETATION

Numerous other theories have surfaced since Freud and Jung, some of which are derived from their work, some of which run counter to it, and some of which reach back to the teachings and beliefs of earlier eras from late-twentieth-century perspectives.

One neo-Freudian dream theorist to base his work on Freud's ideas but ultimately break from them was Austrian psychiatrist Alfred Adler (1870–1937). Once president of the Vienna Psycho-Analytical Society, Adler left that post to develop his own theories and techniques, which became known as "individual psychology." Adler is considered a forerunner of modern dream theory for several reasons. First, his belief that dreams are a problem-solving activity through which the brain sorts through experiences and attempts to make sense of them is similar to some scientists' hypothesis that dreams are a function of the brain and memory (a hypothesis that we discuss later in this chapter). Second, Adler observed that dreams can actually engender emotions that may find their way into waking life, sometimes changing the way we think, feel, or act; in this way, dream experiences have an effect similar to that of waking experiences. "The dream is not a contradiction to waking life," Adler wrote. "It must always be in the same line as the movements and expressions of life."

For the most part, these concepts are in line with Freud's. In a departure from Freud, however, Adler focused not on the latent dream content Freud talked about, but on the manifest dream content—the material on the surface—to see how the dream reflects aspects of the dreamer's waking life. In another departure from the Freudian camp, Adler focused on the dream as a whole, more than on the individual images or symbols, concentrating on how the dream reflects the dreamer's basic lifestyle. For example, dreaming of a dead person, Adler would say, might indicate unresolved feelings about that person that are "deadening" the dreamer's current life and need to be reexamined and then "buried."

Another member of Freud's original psychoanalytic organization who eventually left the group was Wilhelm Stekel (1866–1940). Like Jung, Stekel was more interested in the universal aspects of good and evil expressed in dreams than in the individual meanings or experiences that Freud emphasized. Like Adler, Stekel would concentrate on the overall theme of a dream or series of dreams rather than particular symbols to interpret meaning. Stekel did share with Freud the belief that only a trained psychoanalyst could correctly interpret dreams. In fact, he went beyond Freud's method of using free association as a way of gaining interpretive evidence for a dream; rather, he believed that "a thoroughly adequate psychoanalyst should be so familiar with the language of the dream that he would be able to understand the meaning of any dream without the dreamer's associations." Stekel also was one of the first to write about telepathic dreams in his books *The Interpretation of Dreams* and *The Telepathic Dream.*

Interestingly, not every neo-Freudian theory of dreams goes against Freud's original ideas. Erik Erikson (1902–1994), a leader in the field of psychoanalysis and human development, put forward theories that are more an extension of Freud than a reaction against him. Still, he was an original thinker, and he advanced dream theory in a new direction. Like Adler, Erikson was most interested in the way the manifest dream content is connected with the dreamer's waking life. He spoke of dreams as "a reflection of the individual ego's peculiar time-space, the frame of reference for all its defenses, compromises, and achievements." In other words, the dream is a kind of bottom line of life's experiences, reducing them to their essence as they fit into the individual dreamer's own experience.

Erikson developed what he called an "Outline of Dream Analysis" for examining both the dream's manifest and latent content. In it, he included several detailed aspects of dream analysis later expanded on by other theorists. His model for looking at the "manifest configurations" includes the following aspects of the dream: verbal (word related), sensuous, spatial (space related), temporal (time related), somatic (physical), interpersonal, and affective (emotion related). The latent aspects shared some common denominators with Freud's analysis, such as wishes, drives, needs, denial, and so on. But he also added his own theory of ego identity, emphasizing the constructive aspects of dreams, much as Jung and Stekel had. In a chapter included in *Psychoanalytic Psychiatry and Psychology,* Erikson wrote: "Dreams . . . not only fulfill naked wishes of sexual license, of unlimited dominance and of unrestricted destructiveness; where they work, they also lift the dreamer's isolation, appease his conscience, and preserve his identity, each in specific and constructive ways." In advancing his own ideas about dreaming and personality, Erikson also amplified Freud's beliefs that dreams reflect sexual and aggressive impulses, thereby further cementing Freud's construction of dream theory.

TWO AMERICAN PIONEERS: CALVIN HALL AND FREDERICK PERLS

Although Freudian theory provided a strong basis for dream analysis and research for many years, in time, theorists moved beyond the focus on dreams as solely expressions of repressed or disguised sexual and aggressive urges. Indeed, by the mid-twentieth century, two American psychologists, working from two distinct perspectives, continued the trend that Jung had started in rejecting the disguise function of dreams Freud had theorized. In doing so, these two dream pioneers, Calvin Hall, an academic psychologist, and Frederick ("Fritz") Perls, an experiential psychotherapist, took dreams off the analyst's couch and into the easy chair of anyone interested in exploring them.

It was in the 1940s that Calvin Hall first questioned the psychoanalytic theories of dreams, saying that they were derived from a "biased sample" of subjects, that is, the dreams of patients who were undergoing treatment for mental disorders. In order to correct this bias, Hall set out to gather a sample of dreams from a "normal" population so as to find out what the "average" person dreams about. From his Institute of Dream Research in Santa Cruz, California, Hall collected and analyzed an astonishing ten thousand dreams from the general population. In doing so, he inaugurated a new direction in the study of dreams, now called "dream content analysis," the classification of dreams and what they tell us about different kinds of people. Hall published his findings in his book *The Meaning of Dreams* in 1953—the same year, interestingly enough, as the publication of the discovery of the REM period of sleep.

Generally, Hall found that most of the things people dream about are common, everyday objects and settings, leading him to conclude that dreams are focused more on the present-day concerns of the dreamer than on repressed conflicts hidden in the latent content of the dream, as Freud had maintained. Rather, Hall believed that "there is no such thing as the latent content of a dream . . . [that] a dream is a manifest experience . . . that possesses great psychological significance and that the content analysis of reported dreams is an important tool in personality research." The language of reported dreams (dreams recounted without the accompanying associations), he surmised, is there "to convey meaning with precision and economy to garnish ideas with beauty and taste."

In analyzing the thousands of dreams he collected, Hall delineated five basic conceptions common to everyone's nightly adventures. Each dream, he found, has the potential to reveal the dreamer's conception of the self; of other people; of the world (through types of settings); of "impulses, prohibitions, and penalties" (the dreamer's idea of behavior and restraint); and finally, of problems and conflicts ("the basic predicaments of the dreamer" depicted symbolically through conflict and resolution).

Hall also outlined five central conflicts that appear in dreams. According to Robert Van de Castle, a psychologist and dream researcher who worked with Hall, these conflicts are as follows: the conceptual struggle of the self in relation to mother and father; freedom versus security; masculine traits versus feminine traits; culture versus animal nature; and life versus death. Hall believed that lay people could interpret their own dreams and determine their central conflicts by keeping some basic premises in mind:

1. Your dreams reflect how you view yourself, your world, and the people in it. Rather than revealing an objective truth, he believed, dreams are subjective, revealing how we see the truth.

2. Dreamers tend not to accept responsibility for their dreams as they would for something they said or wrote during their waking lives. But as the dreamer, you must keep in mind that you created everything in the dream, no matter how embarrassing or inane.

3. Because you have many different feelings about any one thing, and these feelings can change over time, the elements in your dreams may shift in meaning. Dreams reflect how you feel at that particular stage of life.

At the same time that Hall was questioning the analytic approach to dreams, Frederick S. "Fritz" Perls originated the psychotherapeutic method called Gestalt Therapy (from the German word meaning "whole"), a short-term group treatment dealing with the whole person. Perls, who died in 1970, is recognized as a pioneer in the field of humanistic psychology, a branch of mind study that promotes personal growth. Perls turned away from intellectualized dream interpretation to an experiential "reliving" of dreams through reenactment or dramatization of them in waking life. Perls was a dynamic speaker and writer whose words were free of technical psychological terms and concepts and alive with the energy of ideas. Here is Perls' dream philosophy as outlined in his book *Gestalt Therapy Verbatim:* "In Gestalt Therapy we don't interpret dreams. We do something much more interesting with them.

Instead of analyzing and further cutting up the dream, we want to bring it back to life. And the way to bring it back to life is to re-live the dream as if it were happening now. Instead of telling the dream as if it were a story in the past, act it out in the present, so that it becomes a part of yourself, so that you are really involved."

Expanding on Jung's theories, Perls suggested that every part of a dream, every detail, every character, is actually a part of the dreamer him- or herself. He described the sometimes warring factions within a dream as parts of the self that are in conflict, and suggested that dreamers use dream reenactment to learn to "own" these parts of themselves, integrating their personalities into a more comfortable whole. (Chapter 6 describes several techniques for acting out a dream.) "If you understand what you can do with dreams," he wrote, "you can do a tremendous lot for yourself on your own." For Perls, outside interpreters such as psychoanalysts who suggest or impose interpretations could not possibly be as accurate as the dreamers themselves.

OTHER EXPERIENTIAL AND ALTERNATIVE THEORIES

Over the years, interest in dream theory has grown, and there are now hundreds of groups of dreamworkers both professional and amateur. As a result, there are many schools of thought regarding dreams, and many of these are quite unlike those of Freud. Some of these dreamworkers, such as Arnold Mindell, actually refuse to even define what a dream is, except to say that it is "an experience happening to a sleeping person." Whatever happens beyond that, he says, is a matter of opinion: "So I listen and look and feel," he writes, "in order to find out what the individual in front of me means by the word *dream*."

Several contemporary philosophers and dreamworkers of various cultures also hold to this experiential or experience-based theory, drawing on the beliefs of ancients who saw the waking world and the dreamworld as merely two different ways of experiencing reality: The waking world, they would argue, is no more or less important than the dreamworld; what is true in waking life is no more or less true than what is true in dream life. Most of these theories are more concerned with experiencing dreams than analyzing what they mean.

Psychologist Stanley Keleman, for example, who has been developing what he calls somatic or body-centered psychology for more than twenty-five years, says that "the dream is not a symbolic or representational state, [but] a special somatic space . . . as much a somatic existence as is our so-called body." Like Mindell, Keleman believes that dreaming is a process that has no value in and of itself, but is a part of the maturing process that he says "deepens reality" and organizes and enriches experience. "To dream," Keleman says, "is concerned with how we body ourselves as adults in different situations . . . [through] the somatic imagination." Keleman's method of working with a dream involves recounting it slowly, first forward then back-ward, focusing on the bodily experience associated with key dream feelings and images, then intensifying and de-intensifying the experience, which he believes gives depth and integration to the dream experience.

Another body-centered dreamwork theorist is psychologist Eugene Gendlin, author of *Let Your Body Interpret Your Dreams*. Expanding on a therapeutic technique he calls "focus-ing," Gendlin developed sixteen questions for the dreamer to ask about the dream. In answering these questions, many of which are related to the dreamer's feelings, the dreamer can zero in on the core significance of the dream as an experience. Gendlin is more interested in the dreamer's physical sensations in response to the questions about the dream than in any particular interpretation. He sees these physical sensations as evidence of "something opening up" in the dreamer, indicating a new "growth direction" that is "expansive and forward-moving," where previously the dreamer had been held back.

Humanistic psychologist and dreamworker Stanley Krippner developed a theory of dream interpretation based on the concept of personal myths. Myths, according to Krippner, are statements or stories about important human concerns that impact our decisions and behavior. Like cultural myths, personal myths give "meaning to the past, definition to the present, and direction for the future," Krippner writes. The function of dreams is to reconcile or "synthesize" people's personal myths with the experiences of their personal lives. If your personal mythology is out of sync with a particular experience, the role of the dream is to resolve the difference. In Krippner's words, "personal myths can resolve polarities and enable a healthy dialectic to occur, leading the dreamer to higher levels of synthesis." For example, a woman who has a personal myth that men are dangerous may face a monster in a dream and through dreamwork see new possibilities for relationships with men in her waking life.

> "EMOTION IS THE GLUE THAT HOLDS THE DREAM TOGETHER."
> —Stanley Krippner, psychologist

Like other experiential dreamworkers, Krippner believes that feelings and bodily experience are keys to the dream's meaning. "Old myth dreams" feel hopeless and draining, "counter-myth dreams" usually feel hopeful and exhilarating, and "integration or synthesis dreams" tend to produce feelings of calm and self-assurance. Dreams may include one or more of what Krippner identifies as "power points" corresponding to the mythic elements of Native American Shamanism: nature, emotions, directions, past events, future events, impossibilities, and ancestors. Like Keleman, Krippner uses the integrative function of opposite feelings as the core of his technique for interpreting dreams. He proposes a three-step process that begins with going to the most emotional part of a dream and associating an early life experience with that emotion, then looking for the message or personal myth connected with that experience. The second step is identifying the opposite emotion of the original feeling and finding an early life experience associated with that emotion, then determining what message or myth comes out of that experience. The final step is taking both the original and opposite messages back to the dream story and using them to eluciate the meaning of the dream.

Another alternative theory of current interest derives from Eastern beliefs and practices. In recent years, the once secret dreamwork practices of the Tibetan Dzogchen school of thought have been made public, in an effort to prevent them from extinction. Dream Yoga, as it is sometimes called, is an ancient theory and practice of dreamwork that describes three aspects of all human experience: waking, sleeping, and dreaming, each of which is constantly changing. This school is concerned more with the spiritual context of dreamwork and dream awareness than with dream content or interpretation; it is more focused on experiencing or "being" than on "doing."

Dzogchen belief states that there are two types of dreams: karmic dreams, relating to the emotional traces of the day's events, and clarity dreams, appearing only when the body, energy, and mind are relaxed and in balance. Karmic dreams are primarily expressions of the tensions or "poisons" of the individual's body and mind. Specific karmic energies or "traces" are said to manifest themselves in dreams related to the six "chakras" or realms of the body, with particular dreams being characteristic of the destructive qualities connected with each chakra. Clarity dreams, similar to what some Western theorists call "high dreams," are often archetypal or teaching dreams that are characterized by lucidity, or the awareness of dreaming within the dream state. Dzogchen followers believe that this clarity has the power to liberate the dreamer from the restrictions of everyday life. Says Tibetan master and professor Namkhai Norbu in *Dream Yoga:* "In a real sense, all the visions that we see in our lifetime are like a big dream. If we examine them well, the big dream of life and the smaller dreams of one night are not very different. If we truly see the essential nature of both, we will see that there really is no difference between them. If we can finally liberate ourselves from the chains of emotions, attachments, and ego by this realization, we have the possibility of ultimately becoming enlightened." These Eastern beliefs are echoed in the writings of Western dream theorist Medard Boss, who states in his book *The Analysis of Dreams*, "There is no such thing as an independent dream on the one hand and a separate waking condition on the other. . . . We must recognize the dream as a form of human existing in its own right, just as we call the waking state a particular form of man's life." Boss encourages the dreamer to consider the dream on its face rather than viewing it as symbolic of something else.

People who claim to have experienced the breakdown of the barrier between the two worlds—whether they are Tibetan Buddhists or Western dreamworkers such as Mindell, Keleman and John Weir—say they feel a profound sense of joy, freedom, and exhilaration from their dreams. South American shaman Alberto Taczo calls this feeling "an immense joy that comes when the house of fear collapses and we realize the possibilities

of our dreams." These theories move beyond the notion of ana-
lytical interpretation after the fact, instead regarding dreams as
meaningful experiences in and of themselves.

Despite occasionally divergent theories, the contemporary
thinkers all share the belief that dreamers themselves are capable
of interpreting their dreams, through various techniques that
include conversation with others. Psychoanalyst Montague
Ullman, who sees the dream as "the world of our inner being . . .
expressed in a sensory mode," has developed an effective group
technique in which people work together on dreams. Using this
technique, the group members comment on the dream as if it
were their own, prefacing all their remarks with the phrase "If it
were my dream" so as to acknowledge that their ideas are subjective, and may or may not resonate with the dreamer of the
dream. He maintains that it is merely a syndrome called
dreamism that keeps us from giving and receiving more social
support from an early age to work with our dreams. He also
blames "the cult of the expert," the belief that only some specially trained person can interpret the dreamer's dream, for our
lack of attention to working on dreams together. No one can be
an expert on someone else's dream, according to Ullman: "We
can become experts only about our own dreams. But we can
help others to become experts about their dreams. . . . The skills
involved can be identified, learned, and applied by anyone interested enough to do so."

We couldn't have said it better ourselves, which is why later
chapters offer a variety of techniques for dream interpretation
and exploration, both individually and with others. No matter
what their school of thought—whether experience based or ana-
lytically oriented—contemporary dream theorists share one
belief: Dreams are worth looking at.

MODERN PHYSIOLOGICAL THEORIES

It is facinating to try to reconstruct the jigsaw puzzle of images our dreams present us in our waking memories, and most people would be hard-pressed to believe that not even one of their dreams has ever had any significant content. Still, what goes around, comes around, so they say. And indeed, after almost a century of examining dreams from a purely psychological standpoint, dream researchers are looking once again at the physiological nature of dreams, just as eighteenth-century theorists in the Age of Reason did. And they are asking some interesting questions. Are dreams merely bodily sensations or impulses? Do they serve some elemental physical purpose, as researchers suggest sleep does? Are they a physical function of the brain? Are they a survival mechanism?

Harvard psychiatrist and neuroscientist J. Allan Hobson suggests that there is, in fact, no unconscious at work. Instead, he says, dreams are the result of electrochemical signals in the brain, which break free at night and cause random images and "experiences" to float through our sleeping minds. Because these images are random, he says, it is of no use to try to analyze their meaning or significance for hidden content. "Trying to interpret the bizarre, incongruous elements in dreams is like attributing symbolic content to the utterings of a person with Alzheimer's disease!" he said in an interview with *Discover* magazine. "You're trying to account psychodynamically for a process that is organic."

Obviously, the idea that dreams are not psychologically significant—that they do not in and of themselves reveal our inner conflicts or desires or other aspects of our personality makeup—utterly goes against what Freud and most later dream theorists have argued. But in his book *The Dreaming Brain,* Hobson concedes that dream interpretation can be useful. "[My] theory does not entail giving up examination of dreams as revelatory of the dreamer's drives, fears, and associations. On the contrary, activation-synthesis acknowledges these processes as highly relevant but finds them, as Jung did, transparently and directly evident in the dream." In other words, like Jung, Hobson believes dreams reveal rather than conceal our thoughts and wishes.

But Freud did begin his career as a neuroscientist, and he was interested in establishing a connection between the activities of our neurological systems and the content of our dreams. Almost a century after Freud abandoned this aspect of his inquiry, researcher Jonathan Winson chose to continue it, theorizing that dreams bear some connection with the memory function of the brain. Through extensive experiments on rats, Winson has found some neurological evidence to suggest that the events of our days are assimilated into our minds while we sleep. The process that takes place during nightly sleep intervals is one of cross-referencing our new experiences and observations with those we've already had.

Earlier research had established a link between survival behavior such as confronting a predator or stalking prey and dreaming, because during both of these activities the brains of animals generate theta rhythms, the slow irregular brainwaves that precede sleep. Drawing on these theories, Winson tracked the neuron responses of rats in their waking state, then monitored those same neurons as they slept to see whether they are reprocessing their daily experiences during sleep. Remarkably, the same neurons that responded to a particular activity (locating a point in a maze) during the day fired off again and again during sleep, strongly suggesting to Winson that indeed he was right: Dreams play a physiological role in etching our daily experiences into our memory.

Does this conclusion mean that, as Hobson says, the content

and apparent symbolism in our dreams is irrelevant to our waking life? Far from it, says Winson. Unlike Hobson, Winson maintains that the things our brains choose to remember and cross-reference are of particular significance to us, and worthy of attention.

Same Dream, Different Interpretations

A male dreamer had the following dream:

"Climbing the Ladder"
Dressed all in black, I climb up a ladder slowly and laboriously. As I get close to the top, the light becomes darker and the space narrower. I am afraid to go on. I then hear a faint female voice from above encouraging me to proceed. I stop, unsure of what to do . . .

Based on popular schools of thought, these are a few of the various interpretations this dream might evoke:

Freudian: The dreamer is dreaming of having sex. The ladder is a phallic symbol for his penis. The dark opening is symbolic of the vagina he fears to enter. The faint voice suggests an unresolved Oedipal conflict (sexual attraction to his mother) that he feels guilty about, as indicated by his ambivalent feelings of attraction/revulsion and by his black clothing.

Jungian: The dreamer is on a spiritual journey that requires hard work and perseverance. The ladder may represent the universal quest for enlightenment. The low light and dark clothing may represent the shadow part of the dreamer, and also the mystery of the quest. The faint voice likely reflects the archetypal Wise Teacher or Great Mother who is giving him courage. This female, or *anima,* part of the dreamer represents the nurturing aspects of the self, which he may be out of touch with.

Gestalt: The dreamer is probably facing the fear of his own climb to success. The ladder part of him may represent the steps on the way to his goal. The black clothes and the darkness (suggesting fear and guilt) are in conflict with the encouraging voice. The man needs to face his ambivalence and complete his journey.

Body-Centered: The dreamer is stuck in his feelings of fear and confusion regarding his future. The dream could be telling him to focus on these feelings to avoid being stuck in ambivalence. The physical sensations associated with climbing are an important key to the correct interpretation, which only the dreamer can know.

Hobsonian: The dreamer probably saw or talked about a man climbing a ladder that day, or was climbing one himself. It may have happened near dusk, when it was growing darker. He may have been concerned about getting home before dark.

WHAT TO BELIEVE

We can't tell you who is right. But we will suggest this: Even if our dreams are entirely random, they still have value. The connections you make as you examine your dream for images that have some symbolic meaning are valid, as points of curiosity, as jumping off points for further self-exploration, and perhaps as insights into the inner workings of your own unique personality.

Western culture seems to have come full circle, moving from previous centuries' beliefs in bodily causes and alternate realities to a newly informed outlook that is divided into three camps: the psychoanalytic, the physiological, and the experiential. The pendulum makes its inevitable swing: What is called modern science finds its roots in the Age of Reason. What is called New Age is really just recycled. We look back to tradition in order to move ahead toward the future. Jayne Gackenbach and Jane Bosveld, authors of *Control Your Dreams,* offer these thoughts on the advent of the growing dreamwork movement in this country: "To some degree, the resurgence of interest in dreams was an outgrowth of the post–World War II baby boom generation. In the 1960s this generation rebelled against what they saw as the rampant materialism of twentieth-century America. They cast off the shackles of organized Christianity and turned to Eastern religions in their search for spiritual meaning. . . . [Now,] the desire for meaning on a very personal level has reinstated itself."

Whatever your motivation—amusement, curiosity, self-growth, spirituality, or something else—as dreamers, you can pick and choose, using your dreams to guide and shape your own theory. You have nothing to lose in developing your own theory or body of recurring symbols with which to interpret your dreams. And there is so much to gain. The next chapter explores some of the possible symbolic interpretations you might wish to incorporate into your own dream scheme.

CHAPTER FOUR

A SYMBOL IS WORTH A THOUSAND WORDS
WHAT YOUR DREAMS MAY BE TELLING YOU

> *I am in some kind of prison, aware that my fellow prisoners are being flogged with a large rubber spider. The guards all look like mummies, with their faces and bodies covered by layers of tattered cloth. I know they can see, yet they have no eyes.*

Is this a "good" dream or a "bad" one? Prison, spiders, mummies—these dream images do not suggest a very restful sleep. But as we've said, there are no bad dreams. So what can be good about a scary dream? Does it contain a message? Is there a hidden meaning? How can you understand what your dreams are trying to tell you?

The dreamer of this dream was curious about what it meant. After thinking about the circumstances of her life at the time, she began to construct an interpretation—an explanation of the meaning of the dream story—that made sense to her. Because the dream occurred during a time when she was working day and night to complete a writing project, she interpreted the dream as a comment on the creative process and how it was working, or not working, for her. How did she come to understand the dream? By breaking down the various elements or symbols of the dream—the prison, the spider, the mummy-jailers—and considering the meaning of each one individually. A symbol is defined as an image that stands for something to which it has some distant resemblance; often, it unites several ideas together, adding layers of meaning.

For this dreamer, in this dream, the spider was not a menacing presence, but rather a symbol of creativity, related to the intricate webs spiders spin. The mummies in the dream, unable to speak, restricting the comings and goings of their captives, symbolized the dreamer's own obsession with her work in recent weeks, work that kept her "jailed" as she pursued the difficult task of putting ideas to paper. Would spiders mean the same thing to every dreamer? Not always. To understand a symbol's meaning, you have to consider the dream in context—in relation to your own life, the culture in which you live, and even the universal experiences we all share. Only then can you accurately interpret the meaning of the symbols in your dreams. In doing so, you will no doubt find many different meanings even for a single symbol over time: A spider may represent creativity in one dream, restlessness (on eight legs!) in another, mystery and hidden danger in still another dream. Only you, as the director of your personal dream movie, can determine what a dream really means for you.

A lot of people enjoy reading dream dictionaries, those thick-volumed books that list hundreds of symbols, from automobile to zoo, in alphabetical order, with a few specific interpretations down in black-and-white. These dictionaries can offer useful suggestions, but don't look to them for the final word on what your dreams mean. Only you can interpret what a particular symbol means in your individual dreamworld. A dog, for instance, might symbolize a fierce and menacing presence in the dream of someone who had grown up with a fear of the animal, but appear as a friend and guide in the dream of a true animal lover. Again, it all depends on the context.

Although no two dreamers will derive the exact same meaning for every symbol, experimental dream research in this century has given us a way of dividing dream symbols into different categories along with some guidelines that will help you to recognize what these symbols mean in your particular dreamworld. Your dreaming mind, as director of several nightly movies, including a slightly longer "feature film" during the final stage of REM sleep, selects characters (and actors), dialogue, plot, and setting for a particular

> "A DREAM IS THE THEATER WHERE THE DREAMER IS AT ONCE SCENE, ACTOR, PROMPTER, STAGE MANAGER, AUTHOR, AUDIENCE, AND CRITIC."
> —Carl Jung, Swiss psychiatrist and dream theorist

effect. The waking mind can then work backward, from the effect or emotion the dream contains to an analysis of each symbol and how it plays into the overall effect. In dreams, you'll find tragedy, comedy, and everything in between.

You may ask why, then, dreams can be so bizarre and difficult to figure out at times. For a moment, imagine you are in another country, where the culture and language are unknown to you. Things look familiar, but the customs surrounding them are totally different. This is the situation in your dreamworld. Words sound the same, but can have different meanings. The people you meet, the places you go, the things you see all appear familiar, but may in fact symbolize or represent other things, people, or emotions. You have your own individual dream language, devised by your subconscious to tell you stories that have special meaning to you. Dreams are valuable life experiences, and, like an anthropologist exploring a unique culture, you can observe them, learn from them, enjoy them, and even come to participate more actively in them.

VALUABLE DREAM AREAS TO EXPLORE

What can we gain from our dream travels? Here are some different types of dreams, with some suggestions about what they have to offer.

Nightmares are frightening dreams that reveal a fear we need to confront or acknowledge. Remembered more often than pleasant dreams, nightmares are defined by the intense feelings they cause, whatever the story line. But don't think of them as bad dreams: Although they bring up negative thoughts and images, they are a positive force in clearing up conflicts. Like the spider dream at the beginning of this chapter, a nightmare usually has an important message to convey, even if it may be so scary that a part of you wishes to forget it.

Message dreams are dreams that convey some information you need about your current social, emotional, or physical life. These are teaching dreams in which someone is usually there to tell you something important directly: a teacher, a news announcer, or clergyman giving you new information to apply to your waking life. At times, a message dream will come in the form of a disembodied voice (with no accompanying visual image); the dreamer may perceive this voice as a voice of the spirit or soul, or of God or an angel.

Healing dreams are message dreams that point the way to better health, sometimes even "diagnosing" a previously unidentified medical condition. How is this possible? True, it may seem like a premonition, but a healing dream is more likely the result of the subliminal perceptions we make throughout our days: our

Healing Symbols

In centuries past, dreams were believed to contain messages of healing. Dreamworkers today continue to find healing symbolism in dreams. Author and psychologist Patricia Garfield says dream symbols can suggest a need for healing some part of the body. These signs may indicate the location of a physical malfunction, the symptom itself, or the diagnosis of disorder. The following objects or situations may correspond to various areas of your body in need of healing. Remember, they may have different meanings in your dreams, whether related to healing or not. The final analysis is, as always, up to you.

Car out of control Fuel tank low or empty House broken into Pain or wounding Breathlessness or drowning	Warning of physical disorder or need for healing
Heat images	Inflammation
Insects	Infection
Water images Weight on chest	Heart-related
Extreme cold	Impaired circulation
Obstructed flows	Blockages
Broken pipes	Blood vessels
Broken pots Shark in the bathtub	Rape or sexual assault

own physical health (or the physical condition of someone close to us, if the dream is about that person), information we've read, advertisements we've seen, and so forth. So a dream of rotting teeth that suggests the dreamer is due for a trip to the dentist could be the result of many things drawn from the dreamer's life: a dentist's appointment card found in a pocket, a commercial for fluoride rinse, a subtle pain in a back tooth. Only you, the dreamer, can decide whether the dream is offering a healing message. As you'll see later in this chapter, rotting teeth could symbolize something else entirely. It all depends on you, and what the symbol means in your life and in your unique dream language.

Problem-solving and creative dreams offer a new way to look at a situation. Because your dreams take place within your own mind, you are free as a dreamer to sort through all the information and feelings surrounding a conflict or challenge, without the usual distractions of daily life. Your dreaming mind can go where it must to make connections with past experiences, imagine various scenarios, or even depict for you the real truth about an issue. There can be real value in "sleeping on it." Problem-solving dreams are the dreams that come after you ask your dreams to help you solve specific problems. They can also arrive spontaneously, as many creative dreams do, in response to your thinking about a difficult problem or perplexing issue the night of the dream. Many significant discoveries and new creations have arisen from this kind of dream—as chapter 7 reveals.

Mystical, visionary, or "high" dreams go beyond dealing with everyday events and concerns to access the dreamer's spirituality. The Tibetan Buddhists call them dreams of clarity. These dreams often include exotic characters who have some universal meaning that is generally understood by all cultures—a bird, a wise old woman, a monster. These archetypes, as Carl Jung called them, often have supernatural qualities, and are believed to represent the powerful parts of the dreamer's personality. We call these characters dream helpers, beings who step in to show you the way or offer some new insight. It is quite rare for a dream to take on the added spiritual or mystical dimension of a visionary dream, but when it does happen, it will be clear to you that something special has transpired.

Completion dreams are another way to "sleep on it," serving to sort out the unfinished thoughts and emotions from the previous day or two. After a completion dream, you will wake up feeling resolved and refreshed, as though things are more in order than they were the night before. Sometimes, a recurring nightmare can become a completion dream if you are able to think about the content and pay attention to its meaning; you won't "need" the dream anymore once you have completed the thought, emotion, or experience that lay behind it.

Recurring dreams repeat themselves with little variation in story or theme. They can be positive, as with an archetypal visionary dream, but they are more often nightmares, perhaps because nightmares depict a conflict that is unresolved; also, nightmares are more frequently remembered than other dreams.

Lucid dreams are dreams in which the dreamer is aware of dreaming while the dream is occurring, and sometimes is able to make choices or otherwise influence the dream's outcome without awakening. These are very special dreams that occur spontaneously for some people, but that can be cultivated in others. (You may recall that the Senoi people of Malaysia encourage children to become lucid dreamers from a very young age. Chapter 6 offers some techniques you can use to develop lucid dreaming ability.)

About Jungian Archetypes

In *Man and His Symbols,* pioneering dream theorist Carl Jung writes: "A symbol always stands for something more than its obvious and immediate meaning. Symbols, moreover, are natural and spontaneous products . . . Dreams are the main source of all our knowledge about symbolism."

Although we can suggest some Jungian interpretations for certain symbols, it is important to keep in mind that Jung himself said that "it is impossible to give an arbitrary (or universal) interpretation of any archetype. It must be explained in the manner indicated by the whole life-situation of the particular individual to whom it relates."

So, what you make of symbols—even the archetypal symbols said to have universal meaning or resonance—is entirely up to you. Some Jungian food for thought:

Trickster—Uninhibited and often childish side of yourself, "cruel, cynical, and unfeeling."

Marriage ceremony—An important developmental transition.

Rainbow—A message from the unconscious originator of creativity, a symbol of the goddess Iris.

Water—Life-giving forces and the flow of feeling.

Bowl, pot, cave, or womb—Container of creativity.

Cat—Contemplative wisdom, independent spirit.

Dog—Loyal companion who guards the threshold to death and helps us across.

Horse—Vitality and energy that is free and natural.

> *White Mare*—Associated with the spirit and creativity.
>
> *Centaur*—Destructive primitive drives not yet integrated.
>
> *Pyramid*—Essence of the self.
>
> *Circle*—Wholeness, all-encompassing nature.

A SYMBOL SAMPLER

There are several different types of dreams and countless ways to portray them through various symbolic representations. Dream symbols have a number of possible meanings, and depend on you as the source to provide the interpretation that makes these meanings clear. It's as though you are the director of your own dream movie, responsible for how your nightly dream story is presented on screen. And as the sole creator of your dreams, you are also the writer, the producer, and the actor, playing all the parts yourself.

Many dream theorists today follow the lead of Fritz Perls and others in believing that all the elements in a dream are parts of the dreamer him- or herself. For example, a dream in which you meet up with your high school rival and take a trip in a convertible to visit a mountain range has all the elements of a story for stage, screen, or television: plot (meeting up with the rival, taking a trip), characters (yourself, the rival), setting (the car, open road, the mountain range). If you think about what each of these elements represents to you, and how it fits into the context of your life over the previous few days as well as the long term, you can begin to see what part of you this rival represents—your competitive nature, your feeling of not measuring up, the social pressure you may still feel. The overall mood of the dream—the main emotion you feel as you remember it—also gives you some important clues to work with.

As you become your own dream expert, continue to look closely at all the symbolic elements in your dreams—the characters, animals, objects, places, and even colors and numbers. As writer-director, you are the one infusing these symbols with meaning that relates to the many parts of yourself. These symbols not only tell you something about your perception of others, but also may ultimately reveal important information about how you perceive yourself. A male character may represent your masculine energies (whether you are a man or a woman), a female character your feminine traits. A child may symbolize the part of you that still feels like a child, your inner child, to use a popular psychological term. And an older person may represent the aging or experienced part of you, no matter what age you are when you dream about it.

Examine dream objects in the same way. A house may represent your own body structure, giving you messages about its strong or weak points, its spiritual (attic) or hidden (basement) aspects. A vehicle such as a car may represent your own (often sexual) energy and how you express it in your waking life: Are you in the driver's seat? Or are you in the parking lot stranded with a flat tire? You can learn to ask similar questions about all your dream symbols, with this chapter as a guide.

Identifying the parts of you that connect with the various symbols in your dreams is a key step toward grasping the meaning of your dream. But it's not the only step. Factoring in the context of your own life is necessary to give you the uniquely accurate interpretation you're looking for. You have the final word on what your dream symbols mean to you. The only dictionary of correct meanings for your dream symbols is the one you devise over time as you look again and again for patterns of symbols and meanings in your dreams. Later chapters offer many techniques for working with your dreams in ways that make recall and interpretation easier, but whether or not you try some of these techniques, you will be able to interpret your dreams with a new level of clarity as you come to understand dream symbolism and what it means for your personal dream-world.

Simply put, it's up to you. Don't let anybody else decide for you what your dream symbols mean—not even Sigmund Freud himself, who would say that every dream is a repressed sexual or aggressive wish, with a veiled meaning that only a professional can understand. And not even Jung, who himself pointed out that archetypal symbols are not always present in a dream. *The Dream Sourcebook* offers some suggested meanings for a number of common dream symbols, but we can't encourage you strongly enough to move beyond these suggested meanings to consider your dream symbols in the larger context of your own life and culture. Use our suggestions to ask new questions of yourself, with the goal of a deeper understanding of yourself as a whole.

Think of yourself as the production team responsible for your own dream movies—the producer, director, writer, actor, set designer, lighting designer, sound director, and prop manager. What elements have you put together to create the movie playing in your dream cinema? As with every good film, each of these elements serves a purpose—enriching the meaning, strengthening the impact, and deepening the total effect. The same is true with all aspects of your dream movies, as you'll see each time you examine one of your own dreams. The guidelines in the following sections can help you understand the symbolism behind the various components your dream theater presents each night.

CHARACTERS

The first step a director takes is casting the characters. And the interesting point about dream characters is, even if they look like people you know or know about—your father, your local nightly news anchor, your grade school bus driver— they have identities in the dream aside from their surface identities: They all represent some part of you also. Your father might represent the part of you that has the qualities you consider to be like your father or fatherly in general, whether you are a father, or even a man, or not. Your news anchor brings you messages, and might represent the part of you that seeks and reveals information. Your grade school bus driver may have made each trip to and from school a joy, with joking and singing along the way, symbolizing for you that the journey of life is joyful, whatever the destination; if that bus driver was strict and unfriendly, a dream that includes this character may indicate that you see the journey of life as tedious and limiting. It all depends on you, your own personal attitudes, and your life experience. So let's look at some of the more common characters making appearances in dreams. Explore all the associations you have to each character, and always consider how the symbol represents some part of you.

> "DREAMS ARE THE TOUCHSTONES OF OUR CHARACTERS."
> —Jean Cocteau, French film director and author

Yourself: As the director, you are almost invariably going to cast yourself as the star. The dream is viewed through your eyes, whether you are a participant, an observer, or both. How fully you are involved in the dream may reflect how active or passive you are in your waking life. Some people are able to experience a dream as both themselves and as another character, perhaps because they are more comfortable accepting the many different roles they play in their waking lives.

Familiar people: These are people you encounter in daily life: family members, acquaintances, co-workers, friends. The appearance of familiar faces in dreams is especially common for women, but both men and women dream of people they know. Why do these people get cast in your dream? As director, you may wish to bring them in to represent some unfinished communication with that character. The person may appear in your dreams again and again until the conflict is resolved in waking life. In dreaming about the character, you may gain insight as to how to deal with the person in waking life. Or, this person might represent some aspect of yourself: A shy co-worker who never takes a stand may appear in your dream to reflect the part of you that shrinks away from self-expression. The neighborhood newsboy may appear to suggest the part of you that has new information to share. Play with the idea, and see what possibilities arise. Here are some of the more commonly occurring familiar characters that appear in dreams:

Mother: Generally the primary nurturer, the mother as a dream symbol can reflect your own caregiving instincts. You no doubt have particular feelings about your own mother, and if she appears in your dream, you should take those into account as you make your interpretation: Do you see your mother as loving? Critical? Controlling? Is there a part of yourself that exhibits those qualities? Because mothers are givers of birth, the mother in your dream may represent a creator or giver of life. Even if you are a man, you have a part of yourself that is nurturing and that gives life.

Father: Fathers are considered typically to be authority figures. Again, your relationship with your own father and your attitude about it bear looking at when he, or another father, or yourself as a father, appears in a dream. Is the father in your dream an authority? A judge? A protector? Even if you are a woman, you do have a fathering/authoritative part of yourself that may be surfacing in a dream about a father or about your own father.

Baby or child: A child is an innocent person in need of nurturing or care. The child in the dream may be your own child, some other child, or the child part of you. Do you have a need you are not addressing? Is there something you should protect the child part of you from? If the child in the dream is your own child, ask yourself whether this is a signal to pay attention to some need or quality you may have been ignoring in your child. Is there some unresolved conflict to deal with? If your child appears ill, hurt, or in danger in your dream, you may be questioning your adequacy as a parent to take care of your child, or yourself.

Lover: When your lover appears in a dream, the dream not only represents the actual person, but may also symbolize the acceptance, appreciation, and integration of masculine or feminine traits of the lover into yourself. In other words, a dream of a lover may indicate your feeling whole or complete, with all aspects of your personality expressed.

Boss: Your employer has authority over you, gives you directions, and provides you with your livelihood. In addition to pointing out something about your relationship with your boss, a dream that features your boss can spotlight the issues you have surrounding this kind of authority and control. What does it say about the boss part of you? Are you the authority in your life? Or is someone else "bossing you around"?

Casual acquaintances: "What was he doing there?" How many times have you dreamed about someone you barely know, only to wake up and wonder how in the world your dreaming mind dragged that person out of the back room and into your dream. Casual acquaintances are part of our life experiences, part of ourselves, in that they may symbolize particular events or times in our lives (our third grade teacher, our doctor's receptionist, a fellow car pool driver), or particular messages you need to receive. When trying to make sense of their special appearance in your dream, consider not just who these characters are but what they represent for you in context. Here are a few examples.

Mail carrier: A mail carrier can be a symbol of communication. If a character of this type appears in your dream, ask yourself how you are communicating with others in your life. Whom do you need to carry a message to? Whom do you wish to hear from? What information do you need to receive?

Builder, architect, interior designer: Someone who constructs a house is creating, giving form to, adding on. Is there a builder part of you in action now? What are you creating, giving structure to? Or failing to?

Animals: As dream characters, our family pets or other familiar animals have special meaning beyond the archetypal symbolism of primal instincts in nature. When you dream of a pet, consider the personality traits you see in that animal, and how those traits might represent a part of you. (Wild animals such as snakes and bears have archetypal meanings that we explore later in this chapter.)

CELEBRITY GUEST STARS

In this age of never-ending multimedia coverage of famous people in the news, entertainment industries, and political arena, our cast of characters can have some surprising special guest stars. Best friends with Cher? Why not. A date with Humphrey Bogart? What the heck. A pickup truck ride with President Clinton? Sounds like fun. Anything is possible in dreams, and after you've enjoyed the ride, you can have more fun examining just what these famous folks mean to you as symbols. They may be someone you wish to be, someone you are jealous of, or someone whose "alliance" or message you believe would be of value to you (for example, "With the president of the United States on my side, I'll go far!").

The President: Clearly, the President of the United States is a symbol of power, authority, and control. A presidential visitation in a dream may also symbolize protection and privilege. Are you taking control or do you feel controlled by someone else? Do you seek protection, or do you desire to be an insider in a situation? Are there general presidential qualities or particular traits in the President in the dream that have relevance to you and your life? You can use these characteristics to develop your own waking personality, enhancing positive qualities and working on less productive traits that you see exhibited in these famous characters.

Royalty: Royal figures are often an archetypal symbol of king and queen, the rulers of your own body, mind, and soul. How are you ruling over your life, or whom are you allowing to rule over it? If you dream of a specific member of a royal family, such as the Prince of Wales or Princess Diana (one of the most frequently photographed women in the world), then consider your own feelings about the characters. Again, so much media coverage makes it likely that you've formed some impression that has meaning in your dream.

Movie star/actor: A movie star or actor may represent the performer part of yourself. What is the actor known for? Womanizing? Political activism? Does the actor seem to have traits you identify with? Has he or she played characters that appeal to you in some way?

DREAM HELPERS

Some characters may look and act unlike anyone you know or have heard of, but become your friends or allies in your dream-world, and may recur in other dreams. We call them dream helpers because they appear in your dreams to assist you, lending their support as you move in new directions, first in your dream, and then in your waking life. You dream these helpers up out of a need for guidance, for approval and acceptance, for care, or for information. Often, an archetypal magic figure such as a witch or magician steps in as a dream helper, representing some crucial part of your personality, such as wisdom, intuition, nurturance, fertility, or spirituality.

In some sense, all dream characters are dream helpers, because they all bring to our attention something from the unconscious that, when examined, gives us more information about ourselves, information we can use in our waking lives. For instance, a young woman recalls a dream in which her kitchen sink was full of dishes and the water was overflowing onto the floor: "Within the dream, I go to talk to my mother. I tell her I had dreamed the sink was overflowing, and ask what she thinks it means. In a soothing lilt that is unlike her real voice, she says, 'Everything is overflowing out of control.' As my dream helper, she was able to reveal a feeling to me that I had been unaware of until that point. I think this helper appeared as my mother because the archetypal Mother is our first and most basic source of information about how the world works, our first real problem-solver and guide."

Dream helpers are usually not familiar characters from our waking lives, however. Archetypal or universal figures are more common dream helpers. An angel, for example, suggests inspiration from the spiritual self; it can also serve as a messenger of significant information. A wizard or witch represents possibilities beyond those that are familiar, including the ability to see past what is "known" in order to convey an important message.

Often, some of the most valuable dream helpers appear in our scariest nightmares or in unexpected or disguised forms. But their presence and actions can be quite a relief, pointing the way, saving the day, and giving us new information we can wake up and begin using in our daily lives. For example, a woman who was working very hard in therapy to deal with her repressed anger toward her mother had a disturbing dream about seeing "a big brown ugly spider." At first, she found the spider to be intimidating, but in considering the dream further, she came to see the spider as a dream helper encouraging her to come out of her "secluded, dark place" so she could work on expressing herself and making more friends. She then viewed the spider as the useful, productive part of nature—and her nature—that it can be. She also resolved to take some specific steps toward communicating more effectively.

ANIMALS

As with the family pet, any animal can represent primal instincts. But because we know our own cats and dogs far better than we could know a bear or a lion, these wild animals represent different things to us, based mostly on our knowledge from books and documentaries, and even from sources as diverse as our childhood nursery rhymes or Aesop's Fables. So look to wild animals to symbolize the more primitive and instinctual parts of yourself. Consider the animal's condition and demeanor: wild and free, caged, docile, fierce. An injured animal gives you an opportunity to consider what part of you might need healing or attention; a literal thorn in the side might in fact be a visual representation of the cliché that should cause you to wonder what is irritating you. Here are some common animal associations:

Bear: Strength.

Bird: Higher spiritual awareness. Freedom or flight of fancy. According to Freud, a phallic symbol related to being good at sex; for Jung, the soul.

Fox: Cleverness.

Ant: Industriousness or insignificance, depending on the context.

Lion: Power, success, triumph. May suggest aggression or fear of aggression in yourself or others.

Snake: Life force, mesmerizing or hypnotizing, creative and sexual energy. Contradictory aspects based on biblical stories include both venomous evil and healing wisdom. A snake sheds its skin and emerges into a renewed self, and so could symbolize rebirth. For Freud, the snake was a phallic symbol.

COMPOSITE CHARACTERS

With your mind free to roam, characters can actually blend together to form composites, combining the characteristics of two or more people in your life. These unique characters, as with any different or unusual dream symbol, seem to be the dreaming mind's way of emphasizing a point or giving an essential clue about the dream. So look for things the characters have in common or where they conflict, and then ask yourself what the message is for you. For example, one dreamer often had dreams in which his camp counselor appeared with the face of his father and the walk of the counselor. As with many composite characters in dreams, this hybrid person represented a state of transition and change in the dreamer's life.

UNIDENTIFIED CHARACTERS

Most of the time, you'll be able to recognize the characters in your dreams. But about 40 percent of the time they will be unidentifiable as people you have seen before in waking life.

Freud would suggest these unidentified characters represent people you do know but whose identity you mask so as to deny or repress the feelings you associate with them. For example, a woman whose father abused her might dream about being attacked by a strange man with a club. Afraid to face or even remember the abuse, she disguises his identity with a symbolic character. Dream analysis can be particularly helpful in addressing repressed memories and bringing them into consciousness so you can resolve them. But don't let your dreaming mind fool you—not every dream (even a dream of having sex with your father or mother) is a sign of repressed memory; always examine symbolic meanings in context as well.

These unidentified characters in our dreams may also represent qualities about ourselves that are not necessarily attached to any particular person we know. So an old woman may represent the crone or wise old woman part of you, or she may symbolize your feelings about growing old in general. Usually, when a familiar character appears in a dream, it points out something we haven't noticed about that actual person; whereas an unfamiliar or unidentified character probably represents some unknown part of yourself you haven't acknowledged.

In terms of the sex of the characters in our dreams, men tend to dream more about other men, while women dream equally about men and women. There are several possible explanations for this difference. Dream researcher Calvin Hall suggests that this difference arises because men have conflicts mostly with other men, whereas women experience as many conflicts with men as with women. Another possible explanation, however, is that women are traditionally more attuned to their conflicts in all relationships. Women also tend to be more comfortable with the male and female qualities of their personalities, which are often represented by characters of each gender. Men, if they are out of touch with their feminine side, may tend to avoid that part of themselves even in dreams.

About Freudian Symbols

Sigmund Freud considered dreams to be the expression of hidden sexual and aggressive wishes or conflicts that our waking minds are unable to acknowledge. Generally speaking, Freudian symbolism equates anything elongated (a hose, a knife, a snake, a baseball bat) with the penis. Anything concave (a cup, a hole, a tunnel, a cave) symbolizes the vagina. With either type of symbol, the implication is that there are sexual and aggressive urges associated with the item.

Here are some common Freudian interpretations:

Bird: Penis.

Bird in flight: Being good at sex.

Snake: Penis.

Unidentified characters: Known people disguised to deny conflicted feelings or repressed memories.

Stairs: Climbing stairs represents erection; descending stairs represents postorgasm.

Flying: Sexual desire; a sexual act.

Falling: Giving in to sexual temptation.

Nudity: Exhibitionism or guilt about sex.

Death: Repressed anger toward the person who dies.

SCENERY AND COSTUMES

Dreams are often particularly vivid experiences, with settings that are as distinct as the characters who appear and events that unfold in them. In presenting a story on film, a director designs a set that fits with the meaning he or she wants to convey, using scenery, lighting, and costumes for full effect. A dream in which you're being chased by a monster might be more effective if set in a dark forest than in a brightly lit shopping mall; still, dreams are unpredictable, and you, the director, may choose to have the monster attack in the shopping mall. If so, you can bet there's a message there. And it's worth looking at. According to dream therapist Karen Signell, the setting is often a clue about when and where an issue that surfaces in your dream first occurred in your waking life. Here are some common dream settings and a few common interpretations to get you started; but remember, it is up to you to discover your own symbolic meanings.

House: A house may represent your own body structure, your basic self. Going outside your house or breaking down walls may indicate freeing yourself of limits. A dream of getting your house in order through cleaning or throwing things away may indicate a need or wish for self-improvement or reorganization of some kind. Various parts of the house can represent corresponding parts of the body or self: the basement (deeper, darker, unconscious sexual aspects), bedroom (rest, sex, dream life), attic (spiritual, higher consciousness), kitchen (sustenance, nurturance), bathrooms (elimination of waste, cleansing and purification). The condition of the house also has meaning. Is it cluttered? Disorganized? Neat? What about your own house? Your body? Your mind?

Water: Water is a universal symbol of mother and the maternal unconscious. It may also symbolize death or a destructive force if it appears as a flood or storm. Running water can also suggest the passage of time or the crying of tears.

Rivers: Along the same lines as water, rivers suggest the river of life and how it flows according to the current of your life direction or destiny. Are you going with the flow or swimming against the current?

Roads: Like rivers, roads suggest direction and destiny. What direction are you going? Forward? Backward? Straight or winding? Note your progress and the condition of the road. Is it smooth or bumpy? A fork in the road might suggest a decision to be made.

Stairs or staircases: Like a road, a staircase indicates direction. Up or down? One step forward, two steps back? Freud saw this commonly occurring dream symbol as purely sexual, representing erection or intercourse in climbing stairs and post-orgasm in descending.

Trees: Trees suggest the tree of life, and may sometimes even assume human form so as to represent your own growth process. Where are your roots? How strong are they? What are you branching out toward? What kind of tree are you, and what specific associations do you have with that kind of tree?

Fire: Fire can represent a powerful life force or energy. It can also symbolize purification.

Clothes: These may represent superficial appearances, and suggest the role you are playing or the attitude you wish to represent. What are you covering up? Clothes may also represent part of your self-expression. What color and style are you putting on?

Mask: A mask can represent how you hide your true self from others by role-playing. It may indicate a part of you that you want to try on.

PROPS

One of the last things the movie director needs to do before film-
ing begins is provide the actors with the props they need to perform the action of the story. Not surprisingly, dream research
conducted in the 1940s and 1950s showed clear differences in
the kinds of objects appearing in men's and women's dreams.
Women's dreams more often featured household objects, flowers, and jewelry, while men's dreams featured tools, weapons,
and automobiles, reflecting their waking life's interests in that
era. In fact, research reported later in a 1991 issue of the
International Journal of Psychosomatics concludes that there
were no significant differences in the content of men's and
women's dreams where weapons and clothing were concerned.
Times have changed and some of the gender differences in dream
symbols have blurred, but objects of many kinds continue to
surface in our dreams with significant meanings. Some common
dream objects include:

Mirrors: These focus on self-reflection, self-realization. They
may indicate narcissism, as in the myth of Narcissus who was so
enamored of his own reflection that he drowned in the water
that was his mirror.

Purse: For women especially, this often symbolizes identity
or security. Lose your purse, lose your power.

Flowers: These may indicate positive growth and beauty.
Sometimes flowers have specific associations, such as roses for
love or lilies for resurrection.

Automobile: Often a symbol of energy, especially sexual
energy for both men and women. Are you in the driver's seat?
Or is someone else driving you? Is your energy at a stoplight, or
heading for the highway? Is your energy parked (passive) or in
gear (active)?

ACTION!

You can almost hear your dream director call the shots. "Action!" And so the dream begins. The plot points may seem downright weird, but they serve a purpose. As with any script, they establish a story line, build to a climax or crisis, and point to a resolution. Are you flying? Are you running? Does someone start an argument with you? Do you step on stage and begin to sing? Forget to take a test? Arrive at the office in your underwear? In about one third of dreams, the basic actions are similar to those we engage in most during childhood: walking, dancing, running, playing. In about one quarter of our dreams, we are talking with or observing others. Sexual activity is another common dream action.

In the past, striking differences appeared between the action that takes place in men's dreams and what takes place in women's. Men still dream a great deal about aggression—whether they are acting or being acted upon. But according to the 1991 article in the *International Journal of Psychosomatics,* men no longer show a greater tendency than women toward aggressive behavior in dreams. Previously, the only known exception to the observation that men's dreams contained more aggression was that adolescent girls tended to show more aggression in their dreams even than adolescent boys, perhaps reflecting the tendency for girls entering puberty and for menstruating women to be more in touch with their sexual power and to have more violent dreams. That women today express more aggression in their dreams suggests that, as society is changing, dream content is equalizing somewhat. Although women continue to dream more about people close to them, infants and children, and indoor settings, they dream about male characters, friendliness, sexuality, weapons, and clothes as often as men do.

Of course, much of what happens in your dreams is unique to you and your life experiences. Here are a few of the more common actions or plot lines in dreams; see whether some of them ring true for you.

Flying: When most people dream they're flying, they feel a sense of freedom as they leave the ground and sail through the air. Indeed, some dream theorists believe a dream of flying is actually an expression of the idea of freedom from physical limitations, from everyday life. Flying may also suggest feeling "high," rising above restrictions to a new level of happiness or success. The Freudian interpretation of flying is that it is an expression of sexual desire. Some experience flying as a higher consciousness, and believe that it can be a forerunner of an out-of-body experience, in which you truly feel as though your being or soul has left your body to travel on its own. Flying can also have negative associations, such as being ungrounded or out of control, or having an inflated sense of self.

Falling: A dream in which you fall, whether down a cliff or simply onto the floor, may suggest the feeling of losing control or having a decrease in physical, mental, or spiritual energy. In a positive sense, it can suggest a very willful letting go. Freud saw it this way, but from a typically sexual standpoint, arguing that a falling dream symbolized giving in to sexual temptation. People often stop themselves from falling in a dream, sometimes by waking up before landing. This may be where the myth of dying if you hit bottom in a falling dream comes from. If you dream that someone else is falling, it may indicate an unconscious death wish, either toward the actual person or toward that part of yourself.

Sexual activity: Overt sexual activity occurs often in dreams, and researchers today believe it has significance beyond the mere wish fulfillment that Freud suggested. Sexual intercourse can represent a positive merging of various energies and aspects of oneself. (If you dream you have sex with your boss, for example, it may suggest a merging of the authority part of you with the worker part of you, resulting in a potentially more powerful, take-charge personality.) A dream about sex with someone of your same gender (a more common dream than you might think) reflects not necessarily homosexual desire, but an expression of greater self-love and acceptance.

When Is a Dream about Sex, and When Is a Sex Dream about Something Else?

Dreaming makes strange bedfellows, to say the least. But sometimes a dream in which you engage in some sexual activity may in fact be about some other aspect of your life.

How can you determine what your sexual dreams mean? Think about the symbols in the dream, then try to determine what they represent. In other words, consider the context.

- ☾ Look for clues in the situation. Are you dominant or submissive? Upset or satisfied? Guilty or fulfilled? What waking-life situation does this feeling remind you of?
- ☾ Consider the personality traits your sex partner exhibits in the dream and in waking life. Is he or she alluring or repulsive? Strong-willed or easily swayed? Could you use more of this personality trait in your own life?

Sigmund Freud's theory was that even nonsexual dreams are sexual. In a dream, a baseball bat might symbolize a penis (Freud called this a phallic symbol, meaning it represented a phallus, or penis). A dream in which you are entering a dark and foreboding cave might indicate a desire for and fear of having sex with a woman. It can be fun to look for these symbols in your dreams, but keep in mind symbols don't always have to have an underlying sexual context. "Sometimes a cigar is just a cigar, as the saying goes."

As for "wet dreams," sex dreams that culminate in orgasm and, for males, ejaculation, the fact is that "having orgasms while dreaming is perfectly normal for both men and women" of all ages, according to Gayle Delaney, author of *Sexual Dreams: Why We Have Them, What They Mean.*

Toilet activity: Anytime you dream about going to the toilet, think about what needs to be eliminated from your "psychological intestinal tract." In particular, dreams about bowel movements can be symbolic. A dream of a normal bowel movement suggests a positive process of getting rid of some "old shit" that you don't need anymore. Being constipated in a dream, on the other hand, may indicate you are holding on to or suppressing some "old shit." Dreaming of diarrhea might mean that you feel unformed or out of control; it might also be an expression of strong emotions you can no longer contain. A stopped-up toilet might mean you are withholding feelings; an overflowing toilet, however, may indicate you are welling up with emotions you need to express.

THEME

The theme is the answer to the question "What was the dream (or movie or play or story) about?" A dream might be about fulfilling a wish, as Freud believed, or confronting a fear. It could concern acquiring something, or letting things go. It could be about your family relationships, or your partnership with your mate. It could be about motherhood or fatherhood. It might be about creativity or frustration. Just as a dream has an overall or prevailing mood, it also has an overall message, one you can explore in your waking life to gain new perspective. Here are just a few common themes to think about:

Nudity: "I was walking to the school bus stop, but I wasn't wearing any clothes." "All of a sudden, I realized I was naked." "Everyone was completely naked, but nobody seemed to notice." Most people have had a dream involving nudity at one time or another, often in the unlikely scenarios these dreamers recount. If you dream you are nude in an inappropriate place, you might be feeling exposed or vulnerable in some aspect of your waking life. Being "caught with your pants down" makes you feel embarrassed, so you might well be dreaming about it as an expression of some embarrassment you feel in your waking life. Nudity might also suggest openness or honesty: You're not covering up your true self. Freud's take was characteristically sexual—nudity to him suggested sexual feelings or exhibitionism and guilt about sex.

Examinations or tests: "I've been out of college ten years, but I still dream I forgot to take an exam and flunked out." "In my dream, I attend the first class session on the day of the final exam, and when I get a B, I complain!" "I'm taking the test, and before I can even read the questions, it's time to turn it in." "I go to take a test and get anxious when I realize I haven't studied and don't know any of the material." Test or exam dreams are quite familiar to most of us. They may indicate a feeling of being "under examination" or "put to the test." They can also indicate feeling judged as to your basic goodness as a person. They may mean you need to examine some aspect of yourself you've been ignoring.

Losing teeth: "My teeth begin falling out of my mouth one by one." "I bite into an apple and my teeth sink in and don't come out." Losing teeth may symbolize that you're unable to understand or "chew on" some problem, or that you're having trouble "getting your teeth into" some issue. Sometimes, it means something is "hard to swallow." Because teeth are associated with aggression, losing teeth may mean you're reluctant to get angry or "bare your teeth." A dream about teeth may refer to growing up or getting older. (Or it may simply mean you need to go to the dentist!)

Pregnancy: "In the dream, I'm pregnant and everyone is happy for me." "I dreamed I was pregnant with a six-year-old child; I found out a week later that I had been six weeks pregnant at the time of the dream." A woman who dreams she's pregnant may be indicating a desire to conceive a child; or she may have become pregnant, which might register with her subconsciously before she even takes a pregnancy test. Pregnancy also symbolizes conceiving or giving birth to an idea, direction, or desire that you have not fully expressed in your waking life. If you are pregnant and dream about your pregnancy, you might have concerns about pregnancy or childbirth. (Paying attention to these dreams has been shown to correlate with reduced complications during pregnancy and childbirth and easier deliveries!)

Death: Dreams of death may reflect the loss of some part of you—lost opportunities, the ending of an era, the letting go of some part of yourself you no longer need. Death of another can represent your unexpressed anger toward that person.

Finding or losing money: If you have gotten a raise, inherited some money, or sold something of value, it may register in your dreams as finding money. It may also indicate discovering something of value—in yourself, in another, or in your life—that you had previously ignored. Losing money in a dream may mean loss, or risk of loss, of money or something else.

Numbers and Colors

Have you ever wondered what colors and numbers mean when they appear in our dreams? To find out, as always, first think about any special associations a color might have for you—yellow might remind you of the yellow house you grew up in, blue might symbolize a swimming pool. The emotional associations you have with a color depend on your own experiences. These common associations, culled from the researchers of several dream experts, can get you started:

Black: Danger; the unknown; hidden feelings.

Blue: Openness; spirituality; a "blue" mood.

Brown: Earthiness; sometimes depression.

Red: Danger, proceed with caution.

Green: Positive change, a "green light" to move ahead; health, growth, and healing; jealousy, as in "green with envy."

White: Peace; purity; cleanliness.

Yellow: Happiness, lightness; intellect; cowardice.

Gold: Value; riches.

One: Individual; solitude.

Two: Partners; twins.

Three: Trinity; self-exploration.

Four: Limitations; earthly things.

Five: A change of activities.

Six: Balance; harmony; love.

Seven: Mental perfection; healing.

Eight: Power or authority; karma.

Nine: Completion.

Don't forget to consider the pun value of colors and numbers in dreams. Plays on words might include sound-alikes such as "one" and "won," "red" and "read," "four," "for," and "fore," "blue" and "blew," and so forth.

You might also be surprised to discover the relevance of some seemingly arbitrary numbers and colors in your dream. One woman dreamed of buying an apartment for $50,000—a number that meant nothing to her until she realized it was the recently reported cost of a controversial magazine kiosk that had been erected in her city.

YOUR OWN SYMBOL DICTIONARY

As you can see, there are more interpretations of dream symbols than there are symbols themselves! Always remember there is no one right answer as to what your dreams mean. Context is essential, and you can look at your dream life from three different vantage points: If you consider it like a set of circles, the innermost circle, the personal, might be the most immediate place to search for the unique references your dream symbols are making to your waking life. The middle circle is the cultural reference point—that is, you live in a city or suburb, in the North, South, East, or West, in the Western World, and as part of a socioeconomic group and religious orientation. These cultural factors are liable to make their presence known through references in your dreams. And finally, there is the universal context, the outer circle that binds us all together through what Jung called the "collective unconscious": archetypal symbols of witch and wizard, king and queen, lion and butterfly, that have a shared meaning among us all, are larger than our individual experiences or our cultural backgrounds, and carry a certain timeless resonance.

The same symbol in two different dreams can have different meanings even during the same night's sleep, so don't think all the work is over once you've figured out what something means in one particular dream. Instead, use the meaning as a clue when interpreting other dreams, and look for connections with an open mind. Don't jump to conclusions! Let your waking mind wander in the same way your dreaming mind seems to, weaving a tale with a symbolic message that can offer insight into your thoughts, feelings, and experiences.

Having said all this, we want to acknowledge that, as they say, "Sometimes a cigar is just a cigar." You don't have to find some deeply significant meaning in every dream that flits across your nocturnal screen. Not all dreams are easy to interpret, and references to your waking life or past memories may not surface at all. As your mind files away the many bits of information it has taken in, cross-referencing with everything it has ever known, some curious plots may evolve. Free to roam, your mind may engage in word play or other forms of humor for its own sake, or startle you with unlikely scenarios that would have you on the edge of your seat if you weren't fast asleep. Sometimes, your mind makes a creative leap so far that the result seems like utter nonsense. For example, someone we know, who had listened to the soundtrack from *Miss Saigon,* dreamed the singer deviated from the powerful lyrics into nonsensical lines such as, "I'm going to wash your car now" and "Have a nice day." Look forward to these nonsense dreams. Enjoy them. They're a fabulous movie, and you've gotten in free!

CHAPTER FIVE

WHAT'S IT ALL MEAN?
A GUIDE TO RECALLING AND INTERPRETING YOUR DREAMS

In ancient times, it took a soothsayer to interpret dreams. Dreams were considered visions sent to the dreamer from outside forces over which the dreamer had no control, and only a specially chosen interpreter could reveal what message those otherworldly beings were trying to convey. While we have in large part abandoned these beliefs, it remains true that most people feel their dreams are a mystery that they themselves cannot solve, and that, while their dreams may not convey messages from the spirits, they certainly don't originate from themselves as writer, director, producer, and featured player.

In fact, as the previous chapter on symbols illustrates, you are entirely responsible for the dream movies you create each night. The stories, characters, settings, and themes are your own design. Sure, your dreams may seem foolish or even inappropriate, but remember that your dreamworld knows no bounds: There are no bad dreams, there are no taboos. In dreams, anything goes. Even if you feel out of control in a dream, you are in fact controlling that feeling of being out of control. What you dream is entirely up to you. Don't be tempted to explain away your dream details because they refer to recent waking experiences; see them as mere jumping-off points for your dream story line. Take ownership of your dreams. Accepting the role you play in the creation of your own dreams is the first step toward understanding your dreams and putting them to use in your waking life.

So you don't need a soothsayer. And although Sigmund Freud or his fellow psychoanalysts might tell you otherwise, you don't necessarily need a psychiatric or mental health professional's input either, except where some emotional disorder exists or you desire special guidance. Though you may work with others and get their input, for normal dreamers, having the final word on your own dreams is the only way to guarantee an accurate interpretation that is true to your personal reality. Yes, that's right. The only way. You are the source of your dreams, and you hold the key to the locked room that contains their meanings. Certainly, ideas from other people—this book, other experts, even your friends—can be useful. And a knowledge of the mythological, historical, or literary meaning of symbols can offer insight. But only you can identify what meanings fit your own dream, which exist in the context of your life experience and value system. In this sense, as Raymond de Becker points out in his book *The Understanding of Dreams,* "No interpretation is ever more than a dream about a dream"—you devise the dream, and then you devise the interpretation of the dream, based on what you feel, what you think, and what you know.

This book may be called *The Dream Sourcebook,* but it is really only a supplement to yourself as the original source. "But I don't have any idea why I dreamed I can fly!" "I've never even been to France! Why would I dream I live there?" "My neighbor is the least attractive person I know! Why would I dream I fall in love with him?" What do your dreams mean? We don't have all the answers. But you do. It may be overwhelming at first to realize that your dreams are a depiction of your own wishes, fears, thoughts, emotions, and imaginings. And it will take a little practice before you are more fully able to recognize your dream themes and turn story lines into meaning. There are as many ways to explore dreams as there are dreamers. This chapter offers several different ways of interpreting your dreams. You can work alone, though you may also want to discuss them with others. As you continue to learn more about your dreaming self, you will discover which technique or combination of techniques works best for you.

Go at your own pace, in your own way, and don't be discouraged if you sometimes fail to make sense of a dream even after working with it. It happens to all of us. Some of your interpretations might become clearer or even change as you become more skilled at dream analysis; discussing your dreams with others can also lead to new insights. Some of the techniques we describe may not appeal to you at all; later, you may change your mind and try them. No matter where you begin, or which techniques you try, bear the following in mind:

C The feelings you have upon waking from a dream or even after thinking about it are important. You can gather important clues about what your dream means by focusing on these feelings and giving them time to sink in.

C Don't feel compelled to analyze every dream. Some dreams seem unimportant, or like utter nonsense, no matter what interpretive skills you apply. Have fun with your dreams and, if you wish, go back later to see if anything new occurs to you.

☽ Make your dream life a part of your waking day. Use the strategies in this chapter to access your dreams, and you may find you have more vivid recall, and more ideas about what your dreams mean than ever before. Let your dreams enrich you!

No matter what the outcome, there is tremendous value in just paying attention to your dreaming mind. A simple act such as remembering a dream and writing it down can help ease the transition from your dream world into your waking world. How do you begin? All you need is a dream to work with. As the producer of your dream, you should begin with a script—only this time, you create it after the movie premieres. Write your dreams down! We offer a number of suggestions for documenting your dreams in this chapter. Keeping some kind of dream record is especially helpful for dreamers who tend to forget their dreams a few minutes after waking up in the morning, but it is actually a good idea for all interested dreamers to adopt this habit. So many people say they never remember their dreams, or that they "don't dream," but everybody dreams, every single night, for up to two hours! So don't cop out. Your dreams are there for the taking. Commit to protecting these treasures and you will be able to foil the dream pirates who block your memory of the dreams you have every night.

> "AN UNINTERPRETED DREAM IS LIKE AN UNOPENED LETTER FROM GOD."
> —The Talmud

WHY WE FORGET, WHY WE REMEMBER

There are many reasons why people forget their dreams upon waking. In our culture, and therefore in our families, dreams are generally thought of as unimportant or silly. Your parents may have consoled you with, "Go back to sleep, honey. It's just a dream." But whether they are pleasant or unpleasant, your dreams are a vital and expressive part of yourself, so don't discount them! Another reason why people might forget dreams is that they are embarrassed by their content. In dreams you might commit acts you would never do in your waking life, and it's natural to put those acts into the back of your mind rather than confront the issues the dream scenarios might have raised. Studies show that people who are good at recalling their dreams are generally better able to confront their own fears and anxieties; poor dream recallers are those who tend to retreat from confrontation. Learning to remember your dreams and discuss their meanings may help you to become a more assertive person!

You probably have a friend or family member who regales you with elaborately impossible tales of adventures in dreamland. And if you yourself are a poor recaller, you may wonder how these images manage to stow away in this person's mind each morning. The fact is, people who enjoy sharing dreams are more likely to remember them. Any attention you pay to your dream life can help to increase your recall: keeping a dream journal, making a drawing based on a dream, acting on advice or insight gained from a dream.

RECALL TECHNIQUES

Ready to begin your dream journey? These techniques can help, whether you want to remember your dreams, recall your dreams in more detail, dream more vividly, work on interpreting your dreams, or track your dream content over time. Recalling your dreams is the first step.

Throughout this chapter we refer to a dream journal, the notebook in which we suggest you record your dreams. If you prefer, you may use a tape recorder; some people find it more effective to think out loud when telling a dream or working on it. We do recommend that you go back later and transcribe the tape into a notebook reserved just for that purpose. You could also create a special dream file in your word processor, and write your dreams down there.

BEFORE YOU GO TO BED

Tibetan and other Eastern dreamworkers consider the preparation for dreaming throughout the day to be the primary practice of dreamwork. Western dreamworkers, too, believe that certain rituals can truly enhance the dream experience. Try as many of these suggestions as you like, devising a formula that works for you:

1. Set your notebook, dream journal, or tape recorder near your bed so that it is within reach as soon as you wake up.

2. Think of this equipment as a friend who looks forward to hearing from you, and picture yourself telling your dream to that friend.

3. As you relax in bed, give yourself a strong suggestion: "I will remember my dreams. They are worth remembering. They are worth recording."

4. If you use an alarm clock, make it part of the ritual. Tell yourself: "When the alarm goes off, I will remember my dreams and record them."

5. Try to go to sleep and wake up at a regular time. This seems to encourage more dream recall.

6. You can make your own dream alarm clock using a tape recorder and an appliance timer. Record yourself saying, "Wake up and tell me your dream" over some soft background music. Program the recorder to turn on at a particular hour, gauging it on a rough estimate of your sleep cycle (see chapter 1).

7. Thumb through your dream journal or read from a book about dreams before going to sleep.

8. Make a note of the date in your dream journal, or say it into your tape recorder; you can use either that night's date, or the next day's date, but be consistent with whichever method you choose. Writing down the date signals your dreaming mind that you are ready to focus on a dream.

9. Put your dreaming mind to work. Try writing down a question you want an answer to that night. It may prompt you and your dreaming mind to pay attention. And you may actually discover the answer you're looking for.

10. Avoid drinking alcohol or taking medication before going to sleep. These substances can inhibit dream recall; however, prescription antidepressants are reported to increase dream recall and intensity. (Indeed, you may wish to avoid drinking any beverage right before bedtime so you don't have to rush to the bathroom in the morning.)

11. Use relaxation to ready your body and mind for your dream adventure. Try tensing and relaxing each set of muscles, starting with your feet and working up to your face. Once you have relaxed your body, give it the message to remember your dreams. Your own relaxation strategies, such as meditation, are other options.

WHEN YOU WAKE UP

These morningtime suggestions may help you to remember your dreams more completely. Try whichever ones you wish.

1. Hold everything! Don't open your eyes. Don't even move. As soon as you know you are awake, try to recall as much of the dream as you can.

2. Even if you only recall a fragment, hold onto it, really focus on it. Other pieces may appear later and the sequences will then link together.

3. Roll over! Shift positions in bed to stimulate further recall.

4. If you have trouble piecing it together, start at the end of the dream. Work backward from there, thinking of each key element, until you can remember the story.

5. If you wake up with a feeling, but no memory of a dream, let your mind wander. You may spontaneously turn to thoughts that trigger the memory of the dream. Often, thinking about the events of the previous day or two can jog your dream memory. Thinking about people close to you may cause you to remember their appearance in your dream.

6. Rehearse the dream. Tell it to yourself aloud (or tell it to

the tape recorder or a member of your household) before you write it down. Vocalizing it etches it more deeply in your waking mind, which is important, because even vivid dreams can slip away after the first few minutes of being awake. The only sure way to preserve it is to document it immediately on waking. Once you start writing down your dreams, you may notice that doing so stimulates you to remember more and more dreams, especially as the process leads to interesting insights and revelations.

7. Throughout the day, let your mind remain open for elements of the dream to enter. If you feel as though you almost remember something, take a minute to let it come into your consciousness.

8. Don't get discouraged if you still aren't remembering your dreams. It takes time and energy to learn this skill. If you have remembered dreams in the past but are having trouble now, you may be going through a dry spell. In either case, more intense focus on these dream preparations should eventually lead to success.

YOUR DREAM JOURNAL

We call this part "preparing the script"—no matter that the complete film premiered last night! You've already solicited the script outline through various dream recall strategies. Now, you can develop it. As the director of your dream movie, you will want to note not only the story and characters, but also the stage directions: lighting, costumes, sets, locations, whatever details you remember.

Interestingly, Freud discouraged his patients from recording their dreams because he thought this would increase repression of the threatening content. In other words, if a patient had had a dream that revealed wishes or fears he or she would rather keep hidden, that patient would "forget" the details of the dream, rather than be forced to admit them in writing. But we know more about memory today, just as we know more about dream content, and we therefore know that you are much more likely to remember your dream if you write it down. In fact, having a permanent record of your dreams can really help improve your skills as a dream director—and as a dream interpreter. Getting into the habit of writing down your dreams also increases your dream recall and will give you even more material to work with in future dreams; characters may come back, situations may surface as your dreaming mind remakes some of the classics (or flops!) in your past.

Give some thought to the kind of notebook you want to use for your dream journal. There are some lovely blank books on the market. Some people take great pains to make their own, complete with a specially designed cover with a picture of significance to them: a spiritual or inspirational figure, for example. But a plain spiral notebook can work just as well. Left-handed dreamers may prefer a top-bound spiral notebook because it is so easy to use, improving the flow of dream images to the page. Of course, if you're in a pinch—on the road or at a friend's—any scrap of paper will do, so long as it has sufficient room for you to get it all down; you can transfer your notes to your official journal later. Still, we recommend that you take your dream journal with you when you travel; in our experience, many people remember more dreams when they are in an unusual location or strange surroundings.

WHAT TO WRITE DOWN

In a word, everything. The more detail, the better. Putting down as much as possible gives you more to work with, and hones your dream-recalling skills for further work on other dreams. Pay attention to all aspects of the dream—the colors, lighting, location layout, size of things, direction of movement, sounds, and so on—and record them, no matter how trivial or embarrassing they seem. They could prove to be quite significant later. Don't pay attention to how you are writing—use it as a means to an end. Grammar, spelling, and punctuation can all come later, as you go back over what you've written (or do not edit it at all—remember, this is your journal, and you don't have to share it with anyone, so you can misspell away!). The important thing—the essential thing—is to get the dream down on paper before it slips away. Even fragments are valid, because they may lead to further recall later.

JOURNAL FORMAT

To get the most out of your dream journal, you'll want to create a consistent format, a way of doing things that stays basically the same no matter what the dream. Establishing a format regulates your dream recall and makes dream interpretation easier. You can also go back and find things much more easily—even years later—if you know exactly where to look for them. We recommend the following format, which you can adapt to suit your needs as necessary:

Date: Write the date in the same place on each page each time. Again, you may choose to write the date down the night before as part of your dream preparation; write either that night's date, or the following day's, but be consistent.

Tense: Write down the dream in the present tense, as though the story is happening before your eyes.

NOT: I was in a big, dark castle. *BUT:* I am in a big, dark castle.

Recounting the dream in present tense brings the story and

feelings to life, and helps increase dream recall by putting you back in the moment of the dream. If this way of storytelling does not come naturally at first, don't worry. Write it down however you like. You'll get the hang of reporting dreams in present tense in time, and it will soon be automatic.

Content: Write down everything you remember, even if they are only fragments or pieces of images that don't make sense to you yet. Much of the time, just starting to write down the dream will bring more of the dream back to mind, including not only more obvious details such as dialogue and plot, but colors, sounds, and odors.

Feeling: Record the feelings you associate with the dream. Note how you feel during, at the very end of, and immediately after awakening from the dream. You may want to underline or circle particularly emotion-stirring parts of the dream, making notes in the margins about how these moments made you feel.

Title: After you have finished, come up with a title for your dream, and write it at the top of the entry. If possible, choose a title that reflects the single most unusual or distinctive aspect of the dream ("Rat-Faced Mom," "Flunking the Test," for example). If your dream contained a particular message, you may wish to use it as the title ("Don't Step on Other People's Toes," "Let Her Go," and so on). Giving your dream a title helps identify key elements and makes it easier to locate your dream in your journal later.

Day's observations: In this section, note any events or thoughts from the previous day that stand out to you. You may not see a connection with your dream right away, but sometimes you'll find one. Usually, your dreams are related in some way to your daily life, and taking time to jog your memory about these associations is worthwhile. Note also any aspects that are different from your waking reality—a house that is yours in the dream, but is much larger or smaller than your actual house, a woman who is your sister in the dream, although you do not have one. When these discrepancies occur, note them and comment on any immediate ideas or questions that come to mind. Stay open to all possible interpretations.

Action: No, this is not where you as dream director yell "Action!" and the dream begins again. This is a place for recording any action you might plan to take as a result of the dream. The action could be related to a dream message, or it could be in response to a memory in your waking life that came to you through the dream. Write down your plans to complete the action, and leave room to comment on the results of your action.

TRANSLATING INTO DREAM LANGUAGE

Once you have recorded your dream in full, you can begin to focus in on interpreting it more fully. You can start by learning a special way of talking about your dream. Based on the theory that all aspects of the dream are parts of the self, created and introduced into the dream by the dreamer, clinical psychologist and Gestalt therapist John Weir invented what he calls "percept language" to encourage the dreamer to focus on individual perceptions and to expand access to the dream's meaning.

We have adapted Weir's technique in a form we call dream language. How is it spoken? It's English, but it's phrased differently than everyday speech. How does it work? By emphasizing your creation of the dream and the perceptions that lead to each character, setting, and action. Says Weir: "As far as I, the perceiver, am concerned, the external world 'exists' only inside me as sensations and images. Objects as experienced are solely the consequence of my perceptual processes." This includes dreams, which he says "take place entirely inside me. . . . They are my own responsibility. . . . My dreams are my own doing. I 'do' me when I 'dream' me." Rephrasing the dream in this way can heighten your sensitivity to the personal associations it contains. You're in the land of dreams now, and you want to speak the native language.

Here's a basic, one-sentence example:

REGULAR SPEECH: I fight with my mother.

DREAM LANGUAGE: I have me fight with the mother part of me.

What does that mean? And how does it help us work with our dreams? If we are the ones creating our dreams, then we are the ones who are having ourselves take the actions depicted in them. We stage them. I stage the fight with my mother. "I have me" fight with my mother. But if every character in a dream is an aspect of the self, then it is not necessarily my mother at all, but perhaps my mother and also the part of myself that is motherlike as I see it, "the mother part of me."

Sound strange? Not surprising. After all, it is a new language. Here are some of the basics to get you started translating your dream.

Rule one: Own each part of the dream by using the phrase "part of me," as the dreamer in the foregoing example did, after every noun (except "me"). You are responsible for everything in your dream—the objects, images, events, feelings. You created them from your unconscious. So anything that appears not only represents the people, things, and occurrences in your waking life, but also parts of you. Sometimes, you may find it useful to break words down into syllables; the background then becomes "the back part of me, ground part of me," potentially enriching the meaning and bringing more material to be interpreted. Experiment with the language, and see what rings true for you.

Rule two: Make all pronouns personal. Do not use impersonal pronouns such as it, that, this, what, one, you. Instead, use

I, me, mine. "It doesn't matter" becomes "I don't matter." "This is really nice" becomes "I am really nice." Doing so personalizes the content and allows you to take responsibility for every element in the dream each time it occurs.

Rule three: Make it active: You cause everything in the dream. "I'm angry" becomes "I anger myself." "It hurts" becomes "I hurt me."

Rule four: Be accountable for all the actions and feelings in the dream. As in the earlier example ("I have me fight with my mother"), acknowledge that you are creating the dream situation by saying "I have me . . . " at the beginning of every sentence and before every verb. For instance, "I have me be confused," rather than "That confuses me."

Always start by using ordinary language in the present tense. Then translate, speaking the dream aloud in dream language, and then rewriting it as such if you wish. You will soon come to see how revealing the dream can be in this state. Here is an example:

"Too Much 'I' in 'Opinion' "
I dream that I publish a brochure. I pick it up to look at it, and see that I have made a typo. There is an extra "i" in the word "opinion."

Translation into Dream Language of
"Too Much 'I' in 'Opinion' "
I have me dream that I have me publish a brochure part of me. I have me pick the brochure part of me up and have me look at the brochure part of me. I have me see that I have had me make a typo/mistake part of me. I have there be an extra "i" part of me in the opinion part of me.

Yes, it may still sound strange. But translating into dream language allowed this dreamer to translate the dream so that she could understand its meaning. She was making an error in the way she was choosing to present the public/published, "brochure" part of her. An extra "i" was extra capital "I"—too much investment of herself in the opinions she held or expressed. Not surprisingly, the dreamer recalled she was often accused of being overly opinionated, and had recently discussed this with her sister, who also had been told she had "too much invested in her opinions." It may be a challenge to get the hang of this new way of talking and thinking, but the results are worth the effort.

Once you have learned to use this language for dreamwork, you can try applying it in your waking life as well; doing so will enable you to take more responsibility for all of your perceptions and behavior. Say you arrive home late from work and get into an argument with your husband. In percept language, you tell yourself, "I have me get home late and I have me fight with Stan." Recounting the events in this way provides a mechanism for taking responsibility for being late, and may give rise to new insights about your hidden motivation for being late; you can then explore your feelings and actions in much the same way you would explore a dream. Says Weir: "I discover my uniqueness by taking ownership of myself and my experience."

One advantage of saying the dream aloud, in regular language or in dream language, is a heightened awareness of the individual words that have appeared in your dream. Puns, puttogether words, sound-alikes, clichés, and words with double meanings are all fair game, though they can be easily overlooked at first glance. Your dreams can often use this form of humor to send a message to you, so be on the lookout for puns in their many forms. A woman once dreamed she was swimming around an island in cold water with her family, only to realize on analyzing the dream that she was, in fact, "in hot water" with them! Another woman, about to confront a difficult situation at work, dreamed of several hand mixers floating above her bed—she was preparing to "stir things up"! Sometimes, a pun highlights a previously unrecognized feeling, as in one dream in which the dreamer saw herself in a room inside a silo—which she translated into dream language as the "sigh part of me, low part of me," acknowledging some sadness she had suppressed until then. Like puns in waking life, the results of dream punning can sometimes be quite funny. For example, one dreamer had the following dream, which contains a visual pun:

> **"Chow Mein"**
> *I am wading around in an enormous bowl of chow mein, feeling very unhappy.*

Hard to imagine, yet easy to picture. When the dreamer explored the visual pun, she came up with a phrase that made sense, "Ciao, Maine." After two weeks in Maine, she was feeling sad about leaving, though it took this dream for her to acknowledge these feelings.

THE DREAM IN DETAIL:
ARE YOU READY FOR YOUR CLOSE-UP?

Once you have written down the broad view of your dream story, you can begin the work of disassembling it, then recrafting it into an interpretation that takes your current life into account. You can accomplish this fine-tuning in much the same way a director might: by going back for close-ups on the people, places, and things that are particularly meaningful or noteworthy in your dream movie. As you focus your interpretive lens on your dream details, you will gain much insight into the meaning of your dream. Journalists are traditionally told to concentrate on the five Ws of a story—the who, what, where, why, and when—and that is what we suggest you do with your dream, with a few slight modifications. Our "five Ws" method is similar to Gendlin's "sixteen questions" method of dream interpretation, which chapter 3 discusses; like Gendlin, we believe that focusing on your answers to these questions can lead to a breakthrough or, in his words, "physical felt shift," such as a release of tension, giving you new insight into your life.

If you like, write the answers to the five Ws down in your dream journal next to the initial entry in which you recount your dream. Or, if you prefer, ask and answer the questions in your head, aloud, on a tape recorder, with a partner, or in a dream group (consult chapter 9 for ways to share your dreams with others). As you work through these simple questions, take whatever comes to you and have fun with it; there is, as usual, no one right answer. This is your creation, not a test with an answer key.

Who: Who is in the dream? Who is the central character or most important figure? If you are in the dream, are you an active participant, or just an observer? If there are unfamiliar characters, whom do they remind you of? Are there any archetypal characters in the dream? What part of you do they represent?

What: What happens in the dream? Summarize the events and actions. What are the outstanding symbols—objects, colors, numbers—in the dream? What is the basic theme, based on the dream's literal content? What feelings stand out? What is the basic feeling of the dream? What mood are you in at the end of the dream? Upon waking? What does your body feel like at the end of the dream? Invigorated? Exhausted? Tense? Relaxed? What situation does that feeling remind you of? Focus on the feeling and where it is located in your body.

When: When does the dream take place? Past, present, or future? Day or night? Are you your current age, or younger or older?

Where: Where does the dream take place? Note the sounds, lighting, look and feel of the place. If familiar, what associations do you have with the place? In what ways does it differ from the actual place you know? If unfamiliar, does it remind you of any place you have been before?

Why, and why now: Why am I having myself dream this dream now? How is the dream related to the events or thoughts in my current life, especially in the previous day or two? If anything in the dream is different from my daily life, why would I change it in the dream? Is the dream similar to other dreams I have had, and why would it be coming up again now?

Once you have considered these questions, ask yourself which of the five Ws stands out the most: Who? What? Where? When? Why? Noticing what feels most significant may give you a clue as to where to focus in interpreting the message of your dream and experiencing the "physical felt shift."

Always remember to take your time when pondering a dream. Some answers and insights may come to you right away. Others can take several minutes, hours, days, or even weeks to become clear. Live with your dreams. And sleep on them some more!

A SAMPLE ENTRY

Here is an example of a five-question analysis of a dream. After repeating her dream aloud, then writing it down in detail, and giving it the title "Letters at the Health Spa," this dreamer answered the five Ws on tape. She later transcribed the exercise into her dream journal, underlining the emotional content, in this case content that brought tears to her eyes as she went through the question-and-answer process.

> WHO: *I am in some places an active participant, in other places an observer. My sister is a key figure,*

*and so is a worker at the spa. But I seem to be the
main character.*

*WHAT: I am at a health spa resort and as I prepare
to leave, I notice there are some letters from my
mother that have been stuck in my door.*

*WHEN: The very recent past; I visited a spa with
my sister a few months ago.*

*WHERE: The spa we visited, though in some
places the lighting is darker than it really was.
Reminder: I want to think about some other places
this may remind me of.*

*WHY, and WHY NOW: I had just returned from
the spa, where the closest friends we made there
were two sisters who were there with their mother.
We became very friendly with them. I think I was
blocking out at the time how much I was missing
my own mother, who died two years ago next
month, and my father, who died 10 years ago this
year. There were a lot of women there with their
mothers. I think it's coming up now because I had
this dream around the holidays. I miss having contact with my parents, which is what those letters
being there and not reaching me is about. I feel a
tremendous physical release realizing this.*

*The message that comes to me from this dream is to
stop and take a look at those "letters," to take time
to "be with" my parents, or the memory of them,
which in fact I have started doing. In analyzing a
subsequent dream, which also takes place at the
spa, I realized I had some further grieving and spiritual work to do around the loss of my parents. I
decided in my waking life to write a poem based on
the dream. The poem turned into a letter from my
mother to me. At the end of the poem, I answer my
mother in a letter that I write to her. Later I realized
that I had the "Letters at the Health Spa" dream on
the exact date of my father's birthday.*

The revelations a dream can bring a dreamer are fascinating, and can truly point us in new directions of self-exploration. Writing your dream down, giving it a title, translating it into dream language, and answering the five Ws are all excellent techniques for understanding a dream. But don't be alarmed if these strategies fail you: Dreams are elusive, and they sometimes take a great deal of work to interpret. If you get into the habit of considering

> "WE SOMETIMES FROM DREAMS PICK UP SOME HINT WORTH IMPROVING BY . . . REFLECTION."
> —Thomas Jefferson, third U.S. president

your dreams from all the levels at which they operate, you will find you have better access to their sometimes hidden messages. For one thing, there is the literal dream content—the actual people, places, and things in your dreams. (Freud called this type of content "manifest," and Jung called this type of content "objective.") Then there is also the symbolic meaning of these same elements—the deeper, subjective meanings, such as a policeman to represent authority, a child to symbolize innocence, or whatever your dream symbols suggest to you. (Freud called this type of content "latent," and Jung called it "subjective.")

Always check your dream for manifest or objective content. This advice might surprise you, given how much time dreamworkers (including ourselves!) spend talking about the hidden meaning encoded in dream symbols. But often your dreams bring to the surface concerns that your conscious, waking mind had not quite registered. Say you dream about your car's brakes failing. You wouldn't want to jump to the conclusion that the dream indicated a failure in your life until you had taken the time to literally check your car's brakes, and considered whether you were due for a tune-up, inspection, or a trip to the gas station! Author Ann Faraday, in her book *Dream Game,* goes so far as to state that a dream "should be taken symbolically when and only when a literal interpretation makes no sense."

Some dreams may have an obvious meaning to you immediately. If, for instance, you dream of beating up your co-worker Bill, whom you feel hostile toward in your waking life, there is not much of a mystery to solve. But even where the meaning seems clear, you might learn a lot about yourself by looking beyond this surface meaning. Translating the dream into dream language allows you to ask what part of yourself you might wish to attack: "I have me beat up the Bill part of me." What part of you might Bill represent? What part of yourself are you upset with? This kind of deeper interpretation can help you deal not only with the person you are angry with, but also with the various facets of your own personality. Remember to look at the dream from every angle. As Jung advised, "It is best to treat a dream as one would treat a totally unknown object: one looks at it from all sides, takes it in one's hand, carries it about, has all sorts of ideas and fantasies about it, and talks of it to other people."

FREE ASSOCIATION AND AMPLIFICATION

Dreams seem to be a wonderful place to let the mind wander. But don't let that opportunity slip away after you've awakened. Exploring any and all related ideas or associations with the many parts of the dream is another way to learn more about its possible meanings. Freud called this method free association, and he used it in a clinical setting to enable the dreamer to move beyond the dream's literal content to its symbolic meaning. Jung's version of this method is called amplification, and it focuses more on the literal dream image than the latent or subjective dream content as the central source of associations.

In free association, the dreamer zeroes in on the original dream image and then, without interruption or suggestion, dis-

cuss whatever associations—other images, thoughts, memories—he or she has to that image. From there, the dreamer
makes further associations to these associations, delving deeper
into memory to dredge up the forgotten memories that inhabit
the unconscious, where Freud believed the true meaning of the
dream would lie. This linear chain of associations leads the
dreamer away from the original dream image and into symbolic
elements from waking life. A typical Freudian association would
look like this:

FIGURE 5.1: *Freudian Association Chain*

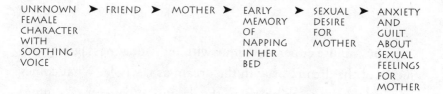

UNKNOWN ➤ FRIEND ➤ MOTHER ➤ EARLY ➤ SEXUAL ➤ ANXIETY
FEMALE   MEMORY   DESIRE   AND
CHARACTER   OF   FOR   GUILT
WITH   NAPPING   MOTHER   ABOUT
SOOTHING   IN HER   SEXUAL
VOICE   BED   FEELINGS
                                                      FOR
                                                      MOTHER

Jung's amplification process is similar to Freud's technique in
that the dreamer freely associates from the original dream image
to other images, thoughts, feelings, and memories as they arise
without any guidance or censorship. One striking difference,
however, is that while Freud followed these associations in a
direction away from the dream, Jung continually brings the
dreamer back to the dream image as the source of more and
more associations, adding to its richness, depth, and meaning.
Jung's method not only leads to reflections of the dreamer's
inner world, but also taps into the universal world of myth and
cultural heritage—often revealing the archetypes for which Jung
is particularly known. Using Jung's technique, the dreamer starts
with the original image, associates it with another image, then
returns to the original image again in search of a second associa-

tion, then a third, fourth, and so on, as if creating the spokes on a wheel rather than the chain of associations Freud's technique creates. Here is a typical Jungian association:

FIGURE 5.2: *Jungian Association Wheel*

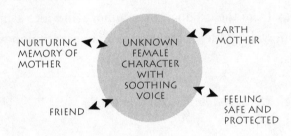

You can use either technique with individual passages or elements of the dream, or with the dream as a whole. What comes to mind when you think about the dream? What comes to mind when you think about the dream's images? Characters? Actions? Objects? Feelings? Don't try to make sense of it, just see what comes to mind.

Of course, these associations are never entirely "free," colored as they are by your own life experiences and perceptions. We have talked before about context, and it is this context—circumstances such as childhood memories, lifestyle, likes and dislikes, recent experiences—that influences the associations you have to the various parts of your dream.

There are three levels to look at when using these techniques to interpret your dream symbols. First, consider the meanings that may be particular to you, based on the people, places, things, and events that are most familiar; these are your *personal* associations. Next, examine a symbol for possible *cultural* meaning: What associations to the symbol are related to the culture or world in which you live? And finally, there are the *universal* symbols and your associations to them, like the archetypal symbols that are shared by all humankind. As you become more familiar with free association and amplification as dream interpretation techniques, you will see that sometimes a symbol has several layers of meaning that incorporate all of these levels. A dream about a peaceful river, for instance, may remind you individually of a pleasant family trip to the Mississippi River in childhood, suggest a cultural expression such as "still waters run deep," and imply a universal meaning such as the flowing waters of life or time. It is up to you to determine how much weight to give each of these different possible interpretations.

YOUR DREAM EMOTIONS

When interpreting your dreams, it's important not to get lost in the details. Just as you will want to identify the dream theme, you will also want to determine the basic feeling behind the dream. As anyone who has ever remembered a dream can tell you, dreams evoke strong emotional reactions. While dreaming, your feelings of fear, anger, love, hate, happiness, and sadness seem very real to you. These dream feelings are another door to deeper understanding of the dream itself. Paying attention to your gut reactions— both during the dream and upon waking—helps to balance any

> *"I'VE DREAMT IN MY LIFE DREAMS THAT HAVE STAYED WITH ME EVER AFTER, AND CHANGED MY IDEAS; THEY'VE GONE THROUGH AND THROUGH ME, LIKE WINE THROUGH WATER, AND ALTERED THE COLOR OF MY MIND."*
> —Emily Brontë, English author

overanalyzing you might do in interpreting specific symbols. Don't be confused if you feel more than one emotion about a dream, or if the emotion you feel in your dream is different from the one you feel upon waking. Emotions are complex, and dreams often reveal hidden feelings about a situation.

When exploring your dream emotions, take time to let the emotions sink in. Don't assign feelings—"In my dream I rob a bank, so I must feel guilty." Instead, just let the emotions flow, and follow wherever they lead, even if the result is "I rob a bank, and feel proud and clever." Don't let your dream emotions' intensity scare you: anger, jealousy, resentment, and fear are normal emotions, and you don't need to act on them. Simply acknowledging these emotions can help you to understand and accept yourself.

A FINAL NOTE

Dream interpretation—on your own or with others—is entertaining and enlightening. But it can also be frustrating to try to understand the story your dreams are trying to tell you or the messages they are trying to convey. By now you realize that dreams operate on many levels, from the nonsensical to the profound. Sometimes, you will recognize dream details from your daily life, or understand the puns your dreams are making, yet be mystified by the message or meaning. Never fear! This chapter is just the beginning. With these concepts as the groundwork, there is far more that can be done with your dreams, just as there will be far more dreams to work with. You have your guidebook for exploring this fascinating realm, so now let's travel deeper into the world of dreams!

CHAPTER SIX

MAKING YOUR DREAMS YOUR FRIENDS
EXERCISES IN DREAM EXPLORATION

By now you have learned some basic techniques for recalling and interpreting your dreams. The once strange and foreign land of dreams is becoming familiar, and you have begun to speak its language. Now, you can begin to "make friends" with your dreams, to interact with them in new and powerful ways that can truly enrich your waking life. Spend time with your dreams, as you do with your friends, and your understanding of them will deepen and grow.

This idea is appealing where pleasant dreams are concerned. But what about nightmares? Terrifying dreams of being chased, being attacked, drowning, falling, dying—these you might just as soon forget, right? Wrong. Spending time understanding the fear that people associate with a nightmare can offer valuable insights into the fears that disturb you in your waking life. A childhood nightmare may remain vivid in your memory and call up frightening associations well into adulthood. "It's okay," your parents might have said in an effort to comfort you. "It was only a nightmare. It wasn't real." But the experience of a nightmare is real to the dreamer, no matter what age: The sights, sounds, actions, and emotions can be horribly immediate. As unpleasant as nightmares are, they can contain an important message about your waking life; you have only to decipher it. You can make friends with your nightmares by learning to look through your fear to the message behind it.

Next time you have a nightmare, resist the impulse to evict it from your mind as quickly as possible. Doing so only invites your dreaming mind to present the same frightening message again until you finally "get it," whether as a recurring dream or a new nightmare with a similar theme. Instead, find a way to work with the strong emotions of the nightmare so that you can examine it for clues to its meaning. Tell yourself that the unpleasant dream emotions are the sign of an important message. Be open to receiving that message. Realize that the dream could have come from many places: an unaccepted part of yourself, a recent scary episode from waking life, or a much-anticipated future event. Use dream interpretation techniques to discern which of these is the source of the message.

Aside from unresolved issues or current conflicts, the causes of nightmares include repressed memories and physical conditions such as pressure on the spinal chord or a brain tumor. Before jumping to any dire conclusions, however, be sure to explore the associations you have with the content of the nightmare; doing so may quickly make the dream's meaning clear. If the nightmares are persistent and frequent, you may wish to consult with a psychotherapist to puzzle through the issues bringing them on. Only after exploring these avenues of analysis should you look for a physical cause for your nightmares. Most of the time, they are nothing to lose sleep over!

A CAUTIONARY NOTE

Remember that there are many interpretations for a given dream. Remain open to all possibilities. Exploring one avenue does not mean erecting a barrier to another. Whether you are new to dreamwork, or are an experienced dreamworker, variety is the spice of dreaming life, so vary your technique from time to time. You are learning a new language, the language of your own dreams. As with any language, you need to use a variety of techniques to become fluent. Learn the vocabulary, then apply it to the exercises in this and other chapters. Speak to your dreams, and listen when they are speaking to you. If possible, discuss your dreams or try these techniques with other dreamworkers. But first, here is an array of dreamwork exercises to add to the basic interpretation techniques described in chapter 5, exercises that can help you to make friends with your dreams, to look to them for support and guidance you can use in your waking life.

DIALOGUE WITH YOUR DREAM

One of the most effective ways to work on a dream, especially one that is frightening or disturbing in some way, is to use role-playing or dialoguing to talk with the various aspects of the dream. The premise is simple: By acting out the parts of each of the different characters in your dream, you can see your dream from new points of view. By putting yourself in the position of each character, you can then allow each character to speak through you. As the characters have their say, you take owner-ship of the feelings and actions in the dream, and you may even discover some new or unappreciated parts of yourself. Fritz Perls, in his description of the Gestalt theory of dreamwork, dis-cussed reliving the dream as an essential part of taking responsi-bility for creating it.

When you role-play your dream characters, be sure to explore all possibilities fully: Don't leave familiar characters out simply because you "know them already." You may not know all the dimensions they represent for you without some further exploration, and there is no better way to get their message than to step into their shoes and speak their words as you created them in your dream.

"But I'm not an actor! How can I stand up and behave as though I am a character in my dream?" Don't worry. You don't have to perform a stage play or memorize any lines. Dream dialoguing can take place from the comfort of your favorite chair. You may not even wish to speak aloud: Instead, you can dialogue with your dream in writing (in your notebook or on your word processor). The technique we present here is one you can adapt to your own skills and interests; if you like, try this exercise several different ways to see which one is most effective— writing, speaking aloud to yourself on tape, talking to a friend, or moving around and acting out the various roles.

Begin by focusing on the dream as a whole. Then, zero in on one character or object or perhaps start with the title of the dream. If you like, visualize that character as sitting in one spot, such as a nearby vacant chair, as Perls suggested (sometimes referred to as "the empty chair technique"). You can switch chairs and become the dream character or object as your dialogue progresses, or use a pillow on your bed or sofa to represent the character, switching voices when you have each character speak. Be the object or character, and describe yourself—your basic characteristics and beliefs. Try to visualize your dream character in the spot you choose; you may want to close your eyes.

Now, talk to your dream character or object (or write your comments down). Tell the character or object how you feel about it, what you think of it, and what aspects of it you find confusing. Ask it questions. When you get to a good stopping place, switch places, and answer your questions as the character. If you prefer, switch back and forth as you go, creating a continuous dialogue between yourself and the object or character. Here are some questions to get you started: "Why are you coming up now?" "What do you want?" "Do you have a message for me?" Allow whatever comes to mind. Don't force questions or answers. Just let it happen. The conversation can end whenever you feel a sense of closure or completion, a sense that you have gained new understanding through the character or object's message. Then, let the "conversation" lead you to the next character or object that may have information for you.

> "IN DREAMS WE SEE OUR-
> SELVES NAKED AND ACTING
> OUT REAL CHARACTERS,
> EVEN MORE CLEARLY THAN
> WE SEE OTHERS AWAKE."
> —Henry David Thoreau,
> American author and
> philosopher

It's possible to really get into this exercise, changing tone of voice to match each character or object, laughing, crying, shouting, even beating up the pillow you are using to represent the character, or comforting it by holding it close. Perls described how to involve yourself totally in this type of exercise: "Really become that thing. Stop thinking. Lose your mind and come to your senses." If you're feeling awkward at first, that's okay. Keep trying, because this exercise becomes easier and more enlightening with practice.

A dialogue between the dream characters or objects themselves can offer much insight into intense conflicts or emotional situations in your life. To create this kind of dialogue, consider which two characters seem to be most clearly at odds. Said Perls: "If you get the correct opposites . . . they always start out fighting each other [in an] eternal conflict game, the self-torture game

. . . until we come to a oneness and integration of the two opposing forces. Then the civil war is finished." Through the dialogue,
you can find out what each one wants, and what each represents. After making this discovery, you may choose to make a
change in your waking life, a change that can help end your own
civil war, integrating some opposing parts of yourself.

Such was the case for one working mother whose dreamwork helped her to integrate a frightening rottweiler watchdog
dream character with a scared but playful ferret from her dream,
discovering that each of these symbols represented parts of her.
After role-playing each animal, identifying their characteristics
and discerning their messages, she still felt stuck, unable to quite
make sense of the meaning of her dream. When she decided to
have the two animals dialogue with each other, she began to
understand. The ferret invited the watchdog to come into the
house to play so long as he would behave. The dreamer connected this resolution with her own need to integrate the playful
part of herself with the sometimes fierce, "dog-eat-dog," working world part of herself. She also acknowledged the need for a
watchdog part of herself to protect the weaker part of herself
that was scurrying around like a scared ferret. After completing
this exercise, she resolved to remain aware of these needs in her
daily life.

If you have a partner or group to work with, consider asking
others to play the role of interviewer as you take on the part of
each character. Free from having to devise the questions, you
may learn more about why you created a particular dream element. You may wish to get up and act out the different roles,
whether alone or with others. And if you share this dialogue
with friends or family members, you will hear other potentially
useful perspectives as well, based on their impressions of your
word choice, gestures, and tone of voice. (Chapter 9 offers sug-

gestions for establishing a dreamwork relationship with a partner or group.)

You might also try having a dialogue with your dreams as a whole. Tell your dreams what you think of them: "You are so complicated, you never let me rest." "I am afraid of you because you tell me things I don't want to know." Then, see how your dreams respond. When you answer as your dream, you might find yourself saying, "Relax—enjoy these stories, because you need to hear them" or "Listen carefully to my messages; they may make a difference." If you are a nonrecaller, invite your dreams to stay with you when you awaken: "I would like to know you and remember you. Can you please be there when I wake up?" See what your dreams say back to you, speaking the words from their perspective. Exploring the dynamic between your waking and dreaming selves can strengthen the "working relationship" between the two, enabling you to get more out of your dreams each night.

YOUR BODY SPEAKS YOUR DREAM

We have talked a lot about the hidden verbal messages dreams can contain, the puns and word associations that so often appear. And we have looked at the way that the present-tense "part of yourself" dream language can help clarify a dream's meaning. But there are significant nonverbal clues in your dreams as well, in the actions of your characters and the motions of the objects. In our waking lives, our gestures, facial expressions, and movements add to the meaning of the things we say and do. It's called body language: Crossing arms and legs can indicate being unapproachable or protective; making eye contact generally signifies being open and honest. We are born speechless, expressing ourselves and experiencing the world through the movement of our bodies, a means of expression and sensation that continues throughout our lives. So it seems natural to pay attention to the physical sensations a dream emotion or even just a word or symbol arouses within us.

To focus on how your body speaks your dream, choose an emotionally charged word, action, or character from your dream. Find a quiet place, sit down, relax, close your eyes, and begin breathing deeply—in . . . and out. . . . Focus on the symbol you've selected. Let other thoughts go. Locate the physical sensations within you, exaggerate them—turning the feeling up and down, back and forth—and then become attuned to any emotions that come up in response to your concentration. When you are ready, open your eyes. What feelings remain? What sensations were most pronounced? How did your body "organize" itself, as psychologist Stanley Keleman would describe it, in response to the image you were focusing on? What is the function or message connected with the way your body responded? What memories—positive or negative—come up that may have been stored in your "body memory" and triggered by your reaction to the dream experience?

For example, if you are choking and feel afraid in a dream, it might remind you of an instance of choking in childhood. The bodily sensations connected with a dream incident or image can be a starting point for free association that may lead to some important realizations. Let your feelings be your guide; they can help you identify the key to the meaning of your dream by creating what Eugene Gendlin, author of *Let Your Body Interpret Your Dreams,* calls the "felt body shift"—that feeling of "Aha!" that comes from acquiring new information.

You might wish to add some comments about this exercise to your dream journal entry. The results may be quite healing, as they were for a woman who was dealing with the recent death of her mother and had a dream in which she called her mother

"Sweetie." In focusing on her physical response to that word alone, she began to feel a physical sensation of heaviness in her chest that recalled her grief ("heavy heart"), leading to a new level of understanding and completion about her mother and her loss.

Another way to focus on and utilize the nonverbal aspects of your dreams is to act them out physically in movement or dance. Dreams have inspired so much creative expression over the centuries that it is not surprising that dance and movement can take their inspiration from them. Just as our gestures and expressions have meaning, so can our dance impulses. Let your dream emotions guide you through this exercise. Don't worry about being a good dancer—whatever movement you create will be the right one for you. No one is watching. Let yourself go!

Begin by concentrating fully on one of the characters or objects from your dream. You might do the dialogue exercise first, as a way of getting to know the dream symbol you've chosen, or you might choose instead to simply empty your mind of all else and focus or meditate on the image itself. Slowly begin to move in response to your feelings. Continue to move, exaggerating your movements, allowing them to pull you. Give yourself over to the feeling of moving to the mood your dream evokes. Do not judge or analyze your movement. Simply move with it until you feel you have completed the movement.

Your movements need not be like choreographed "dancing"—just let them flow from your feelings or from an association you have with the dream. One woman used movement to gain insight into the following dream: "I am running to catch a bus—No. 30. I stop one bus in the middle of the street, but the annoyed bus driver tells me it's not No. 30. I keep running, but there is no bus No. 30. A man stops his car to offer me a ride. I get in and he moves closer to me, asking me to stay with him

I say no, and begin to get upset." To learn more about this dream, she went outside to try it out in movement. After running a short distance as if running for the bus, she felt the urge to run in place, exerting effort yet going nowhere. Finally, in a burst of energy, she ran across the yard. In thinking about the movement experience, she realized that the number thirty to her represented the age of thirty, when she ended a marriage and became "unstuck." The message of the dream, she thought, was that she could move on energetically to new challenges, rather than waiting around for someone to take her where she was going.

ART AS INTERPRETATION

Another nonverbal approach to dreamwork is creating art based on your dream images. You don't have to be an "artist" to create meaningful work based on your dreams. This technique is suitable for everyone, and can help you to notice more details of the dream, bring out more feelings, and give you a sense of control and ownership. Children, especially, get a sense of mastery over the frightening images in their dreams by drawing the elements they can't quite put into words. Whatever your age, if you feel you cannot describe in words what you see in a dream, this technique may work especially well, freeing you from the constraints words sometimes impose.

Use the pages of your dream journal (or a separate sheet of paper) as your canvas, drawing pictures of dream characters, objects, and scenes. You need not depict everything in the dream. Instead, choose a subject or image that lends itself to a rendering. Focus intently on it and notice what feelings emerge. Don't worry about whether you are artistic or not; this exercise is just for you. If stick figures work for you, then use them! The important thing is to put down on paper the things that you

FIGURE 6.1: *This is a drawing by co-author Phyllis Koch-Sheras called* The Triad *that took its inspiration from a dream about how she and her two collaborators could support each other during the writing of her previous book.*

observe in your dream. If you like, you can do a series of drawings featuring different characters and scenarios in the dream.

You might also try enclosing the drawing in an outline of a body, so as to emphasize the connection of the dream to your own body and inner self. (To make it even more graphic, get a large piece of paper and have a friend trace an outline of your body onto it!) In these drawings, place your dream images in various locations within the body, then examine where you put them to see what meanings become evident. One man made a dream body drawing after knee reconstruction surgery and noticed he had drawn the evergreen tree in his dream directly over the healing knee. He also noticed a feeling of healing while coloring the tree deep green, and that, after finishing the drawing, his knee felt much better!

As you work on your drawing, note whether any forgotten dream fragments or new feelings now surface. Spend some time thinking about the drawing. What did you put in? What did you leave out? Which element is prominent? Which is in the background? What colors did you use? Do they suggest a particular mood or association? (Scan through chapter 4 to see what the objects in your dream might symbolize.) You may want to put up your dream drawing where you can see it, think about it, and dream about it some more.

You might also try recreating the objects in your dreams, choosing a symbol and making it as a reminder of the dream. You could simply buy the item or have it made for you, but it will probably mean more if you make it yourself. After all, you made the dream to begin with! When Phyllis Koch-Sheras was writing her previous dream book, *Dream On: A Dream Interpretation and Exploration Guide for Women,* she did this with a dream about a sculpture. Never having sculpted before, she used clay to recreate an image from her dream in a sculpture called *The Triad,* which featured herself and her two co-authors. She made a drawing first, but "the real thrill came," she says, "when I made the sculpture and could *feel* the differences between the three characters in the dream. It was also exciting to discover a new form of self-expression, one that I will never forget." (Her drawing of the sculpture is featured on page 145.)

MAKING A DREAM SHIELD
OR DREAM MANDALA

A dream shield or dream mandala is rather like a family crest for your dreams. Both of these feature special symbols from one or several of your dreams, enclosed in a circular border. The circle shape is often seen to symbolize the wholeness of human nature—think of the zodiac, of circle dances, and of ritual stone circles such as Stonehenge. You might think of the circle as a container for your sometimes disturbing dream images, a place to contain them safely, for even though they are sometimes scary, they are important to look at. A mandala is a circular design that, in Hinduism and Buddhism, symbolizes wholeness or unity; the dream mandala is similarly symbolic, representing the whole of your dream story. The dream shield derives from Native American tradition, which included the creation of a ceremonial shield to represent sacred community and personal identity. Every person in a tribe had a shield of some kind which, as described in the book *Seven Arrows,* "told who the man was, what he sought to be, and what his loves, fears, and dreams were. Almost everything about him was written there, reflected in the Mirror of his Shield."

The elements in your dream shield or mandala should have special meaning for you, drawn from your significant dream experiences and their relation to your waking life; you can focus on one dream, or draw on recurring or memorable images from several dreams. Often, a dream shield or mandala will include archetypal images or dream helpers. You might want to incubate a dream for guidance in choosing which symbols to include. You can post the dream shield or mandala near your bed, as an icon to promote dreaming, or share it with a friend or fellow dream lover. (See page 148 for an example of a dream shield.)

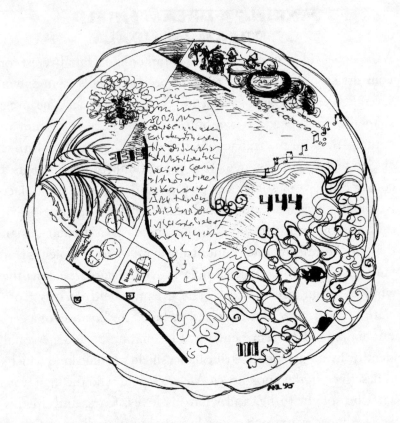

FIGURE 6.2: *Co-author Amy Lemley created this dream shield based on elements that appear frequently in her dreams. The golden-haired woman is a singer, whose songs are unlike any the dreamer has heard while awake. The map, to the left, and the open passport above it are other frequent dream subjects, symbolizing travel (she often dreams she has lost or forgotten her passport). Many of her dreams concern shopping, often in antique or thrift stores, always in shops filled with item after item too remarkable to describe. Some recent dreams have involved minnows spilling out from her new palm trees, pictured at left, and her dog, whose face appears at the top of the shield.*

CREATE A SPECIAL DREAM SPACE

In many cultures, rituals of sleep and dreams are sacred. You, too, can create a dream environment or special "dream space" for yourself. Taking care with your surroundings encourages better recall and more productive dreams. Here are some tips:

C Meditate on your dream shield before you go to sleep.

C Wear a special piece of comfortable sleepwear. If a particular color appears often in your dreams, you could choose to wear something of that color.

C Wear a charm that symbolizes some aspect of your dreaming self.

C Hang a dream catcher near your bed like Native American dreamers do. You can even make it yourself.

C Put a bulletin board near your bed where you can post dream drawings or dream-inspired writings.

C Make a dream pillow. Stuff a sachet with mugwort, traditionally called the "dream herb" because it is believed to stimulate dream recall and add to the intensity of the dream experience. Other aromatic herbs also can be mixed with stuffing and sewn into a pillow to stimulate recall (see "Herbal Dream Blends," page 187).

C Choose a particular set of sheets or a dream blanket that you associate with dreaming.

◖ Try sleeping in a different place on nights set aside for experimental dreaming purposes. Some people enjoy camping out on nights they wish to have special dreams.

Make Your Own Dream Catcher

Native Americans use dream catchers to filter out nightmares and draw in pleasant dreams. These hand-crafted items have become popular in recent years as interest in Native American customs has grown, and are available for sale in many gift shops and stores that feature Western artifacts. Although traditional dream catchers were plain and unadorned, save for a feather showing good dreams where they could enter, contemporary ones are often quite decorative.

To make your own dream catcher, visit a craft store to obtain a circular metal base, some scraps of leather or cloth, some leather laces, and whatever feathers and beads strike your fancy. (Some craft stores sell dream catcher kits.)

Bind the metal base so that it is completely covered with the scraps, using the laces to hold the scraps in place. Next, create a large grid pattern of laces across the circle in both directions (think of a very primitive, large-scale tennis racket). Create a loop for hanging, then begin to decorate, attaching feathers and beads in a design that pleases you.

Hang your dream catcher in a specially chosen place, preferably near your bed, and dream on!

YOUR DREAM WORLD SERIES

After you have spent some time on dreamwork, you begin to see that certain themes and symbols recur, even in dreams about different topics. These symbols usually have the same meaning, or a very similar one, even though the dream stories may be different. Examining your dreams in a series and looking for continuity of symbols can shed light on the baffling images in your dreams and on the difficult conflicts or transitions in your waking life. And discovering changes in your recurring dream symbols and themes is clear evidence of evolution in your waking life. For this reason, some dream enthusiasts enjoy reading over their past year's dream journal entries as a rite of passage on their birthdays. New Year's Day is another symbolic day to engage in this ritual.

One man uncovered some interesting things about his personal development when he examined a lifetime of flying dreams as a series, exploring their changing themes from childhood through middle age. He comments:

> *They started occurring during dreams when I was being chased. I would jump, and instead of just landing five or six feet down the pavement, I would kind of glide in the air. I remember these dreams as getting away from something frightening. But some of them focused on moving toward someone, such as catching up with my friends. Later, I would dream that I was curious about something on the other side of a wall or building, and I would fly over there and hover as I explored. Eventually, I would travel to places far away, but within the line of sight: a building in the distance, a park, or the shore across the bay on Long Island Sound. As I got older, the dreams would carry with them a different feature—I would be going to high places and*

*the flying would involve transporting myself to a
place where I could observe people or events. When
I look at these dreams in a series over time, I see
that they parallel my actual experience of aging.
They shifted from primarily a kinesthetic experience to a more social and strategic tool through
which I could do things and learn things.*

As you continue with your dreamwork, you may notice
recurring themes—forgetting something, escaping from danger,
committing a heroic act, battling nature—in your own nightly
adventures. Whether the series occurs in short succession or over
a period of years, exploring the evolution of the theme might
shed light on your own personal development.

FINISHING OR CHANGING YOUR DREAMS

Sometimes, our dreams leave us with a sense of anxiety or
"unfinished business." Other times, we literally do not get to finish our dreams because an alarm, a barking dog, or a crying
baby wakes us up. It's like having to walk out of a movie in the
middle of the pivotal scene. Can you finish an unfinished dream?
There are many ways to do so, the easiest of which is to do nothing; the dream themes of an unfinished dream often recur spontaneously over the following few nights. But you might prefer to
work actively toward resolution, especially if it is a disturbing
dream or a nightmare that keeps recurring; once you complete
the dream, it will stop returning to bother you. Here are some
techniques to try:

Replay: This strategy is a way of promoting the dreaming
mind's natural inclination to go back over the interrupted material. Before you fall asleep the next night, go over the dream in
detail, and tell yourself you will complete the dream that night.
Continue to do so each night until the dream feels finished. Keep

in mind, however, that you may not revisit the same theme through the exact same story line and characters; the dream may get resolved through an alternative form. Work with your dreams during the week following the unfinished dream, with an eye toward finding related themes.

Waking fantasy: Begin by relaxing completely. Let your body feel loose and restful as your mind unwinds. If you wish, close your eyes. When you feel fully relaxed, begin to replay the dream in your mind. See it as clearly and vividly as you can. Go over every detail and strive to feel the feelings the dream originally provoked. Whether narrating it in your mind or aloud to a friend or group, stay in the present tense: "I am walking down a long hallway. My face feels very cold," and so forth. When you get to the part where you woke up, or where the dream ended prematurely for whatever reason, allow yourself to continue the narrative. Let it flow—don't worry about whether you "really dreamed this." Think of it as a waking dream, and follow it wherever it leads you. Continue until you feel you have come to the end.

Changing your dream: Sometimes a dream is so upsetting that you would like to forget it, before you even take the time to understand what it might mean. The Senoi people called the disturbing images in dreams "the evil spirits of the dream universe." To confront and change these evil spirits into dream helpers, turn the negative into the positive. Because this is your dream, you want to be in control of it: When changing a dream, confront your oppressors, right the wrongs, and take command of your dreamworld for the better. Use dream dialogues to converse with the elements of your dream that disturb you, then engage in waking fantasy to amend the story to match your own wishes and desires. You may wish to begin by asking questions such as: "Who are you?" "Why are you coming up now?"

"What do you want from me?" "What is the source of your power?" "What gift do you have for me?" When you have begun to understand the message, change the figure or the story so that you are in control of your dream's direction and outcome.

You can also modify or destroy the negative images in your dreams. First, be sure you have received everything from them that you need; don't just change them to avoid confronting difficult issues or aspects of yourself. Focus on them for a few minutes, get their message, keep the useful parts of them, then say good-bye, and, in waking fantasy, burn, bomb, kill, melt, or otherwise eliminate the offending images. Tell them they are gone, and that you forgive them, if necessary, but that they are not needed or welcome to come back to your dreamworld—at least not in that form. For example, you might kill off your negative dream Mother, but bring her back into your dreams or fantasy work in a new, more positive way. You can think of this as a way of letting go of or changing a part of you that is no longer useful.

One woman singer used this technique to rework a negative dream experience into one that was helpful and positive. In her dream, she is working on learning the musical score to *Fiddler on the Roof*, part of which was sung at her wedding, with several other people and discovers that all of the solos have already been assigned; she becomes nervous and upset, and says, "It's not fair!" She connected the dream with her wedding and recent divorce. Rather than feel like there were no "solos" out there for her, she chose to change the ending of the dream, fantasizing a bonfire in which she and her colleagues burn the score, and she proceeds to write her own script and sing a solo of her own. Determining that she didn't need the old "score" (or the marriage) any longer helped her to move on alone ("solo") and create a new life script.

LUCID DREAMING

Have you ever found yourself in the middle of a dream, aware that you're dreaming and perhaps able to make choices and take actions that affect the dream's outcome without waking up? Awareness of this kind is called lucid dreaming, and it seems to be little known in our culture. In other cultures, however, lucid dreaming is a prized skill, and dreamworkers around the world have for centuries cultivated this practice as a way of getting the most out of their dreams each night. In these societies, dream manipulations are believed to be more effectively practiced during the dream state, where we are free of the limitations of our physical bodies. Buddhism, Taoism, Hinduism, and Sufism are among the cultures that have valued lucid dreaming through the ages. Greek philosopher Aristotle, too, made reference in his writings to the "consciousness" of a dream taking place during sleep. In 1876, the Marqis d'Hervey Saint-Denys published *Dreams and How to Guide Them,* becoming the first Western dreamworker to discuss lucid dreaming as a practice. A lifelong dream experimenter, Saint-Denys developed ways to manipulate his dreams while in the dream state.

It was a Dutch psychiatrist named Frederick Van Eeden who in 1913 coined the term lucid dreaming in the "Proceedings of the Society for Psychical Research." At the time, however, most people were looking at either the progress of physical science or the theories of Freud, who did not advocate tampering with the messages of the unconscious except to analyze them. So, Van Eeden's observations went relatively unnoticed until they were reprinted in 1969 in psychologist Charles Tart's *Altered States of Consciousness.* Since that time, many modern researchers have studied this phenomenon to such an extent that some say the study of lucid dreaming is now dominating the field of dream research.

Everyone has probably had a lucid dream at one time or another. For most people, lucidity commonly occurs during a nightmare, when they suddenly realize that the frightening experience is taking place in a dream rather than in waking life. Sometimes, this awareness is enough to relieve the fear, and the dream continues, without the dreamer awakening. But often, the dreamer wakes up soon after becoming lucid. For those who seek out lucid dreams, the goal is to remain lucid in the dream, directing and controlling the experience without waking up.

> *"I DO NOT KNOW WHETHER I WAS THEN A MAN DREAMING I WAS A BUTTERFLY, OR WHETHER I AM NOW A BUTTERFLY DREAMING I AM A MAN."*
> —*Chuang Tzu, Chinese philosopher*

It's possible, even desirable, to have a pleasant lucid dream, in which you are able to participate in the events, influencing the story or altering characters as you wish. This type of dream is a wonderful experience. Flying is a typical scenario for a lucid dream. Perhaps because flying is such an unusual and exhilarating experience, and one that no one has during waking life, dreamers often realize they are dreaming after they take flight in dreams. But seasoned lucid dreamers might become lucid first, then choose to include flying as part of the dream. Anyone who has had a pleasurable flying dream can understand why—the feeling of freedom and excitement is unforgettable. Lucid dreamers report that their lucid dreams are unusually thrilling, filled with emotions and colors far more intense than those of regular dreams. "It's not that I have lucid dreams that often," said one dreamer after recounting several lucid dreams. "It's just that my lucid dreams are so memorable."

Lucid dreams are hard to get the hang of, perhaps because the experience of dream awareness is so startling and unfamiliar. Most dreamers have a difficult time staying lucid once it occurs to them that they are dreaming. "Hey, wait a minute! This must be a dream!" is a thought that is often followed by the impulse to wake up, or an uncontrollable tendency to slip back into the usual "unaware" dream state. In *Control Your Dreams*, their comprehensive book on lucid dreaming, authors Jayne Gackenbach and Jane Bosveld describe this "profoundly different reality" as "another world that bridges waking and sleeping consciousness. You are 'in' the dream *and* 'outside' of it all at once . . . [which] can create both confusion and curiosity" that sometimes causes you to awaken or switch gears and lose hold of the awareness. With practice, however, you can learn to hold on to lucidity.

If you want to experience a lucid dream, plan ahead. Think about what you would like to gain from lucid dreaming, and what you would like to have happen when you become lucid. Flying is a wonderful place to start. So is making love, meeting up with a long-lost friend or relative, or discovering some unknown talent. You can also take the opportunity to receive a valuable gift or an important piece of information from your dream or a character in it. You could also plan to learn more about a puzzling or disturbing image from a previous dream. Looking forward to lucidity will help you to remain in the dream state after you realize what is going on.

Many contemporary dream researchers have developed methods for inducing lucid dreaming. These techniques include focusing on the dreamlike images that appear just before falling asleep (the hypnogogic dreams) and also suggesting to yourself at bedtime that you will become lucid when you notice anything inconsistent or improbable in a dream. Dream incubation is a good strategy to employ if you're interested in lucid dreaming, you can use it to "program" yourself to remain in the dream once you realize you are dreaming. Dream researcher Steven

Laberge devised a technique he calls mnemonic induction of lucid dreams, or MILD, in which dreamers prompt themselves to awaken after a dream and focus on the dream details, especially the inconsistencies. They then tell themselves to become lucid after returning to sleep, especially if an inconsistency or "dream sign" appears. Laberge maintains that this technique is most effective when used with such technological devices as his "dreamlight goggles," which detect rapid eye movement and trigger a light that alerts the sleeping subject to the onset of dreaming.

Another lucid dreaming technique involves what German psychologist Paul Tholey and others call critical state testing, which involves asking yourself during the day if you are dreaming, particularly in situations that in some way remind you of a dream. Asking yourself "Am I dreaming?" when these situations arise should then lead to a similar testing process during the dream state, and therefore, hypothetically, to lucid dreaming. (Be careful what kind of suggestion you give yourself. One dreamworker repeatedly instructed himself to "wake up during my dreams," and found that he would awaken several times a night! The dreaming mind can be quite literal, so state your instructions exactly.) You may not need to tell yourself to begin lucid dreaming. Sometimes, meditating or merely paying more attention to dreams in your waking life is enough to bring on more frequent lucid dreaming.

Many people learned of these and similar techniques for inducing lucid dreaming from Carlos Castaneda's popular novel *Journey to Ixtlan,* published in 1972. In the book, the character Don Juan, who is a sorcerer, offers these instructions: "Pick one thing in advance [such as your hands] and find it in your dreams; this will awaken consciousness within the dream." Remembering to "look" at them during the dream, he said, would serve as a cue that signaled that a dream was taking place. Other of Castaneda's books, among them *The Teachings of Don Juan, A Separate Reality,* and, most recently, *The Art of Dreaming,* have brought the ancient traditions of the South American shaman into general awareness; in these novels, he promotes the belief that the dreamworld is simply another dimension of human experience, and that we can access it more effectively through certain practices. While scientists have verified the effectiveness of some of the techniques he discusses—the hand cue we describe is one that reportedly works—the fact that Castaneda bases his writings on his experiences alone and not on research detracts somewhat from the books' validity, according to some reviewers. Nonetheless, he has a large following of people who try to incorporate his teachings into their lives.

> "*WHAT DREAMING DOES IS GIVE US THE FLUIDITY TO ENTER INTO OTHER WORLDS BY DESTROYING OUR SENSE OF KNOWING THIS WORLD . . . . DREAMING [IS] A JOURNEY OF UNTHINKABLE DIMENSIONS, A JOURNEY THAT, AFTER MAKING US PERCEIVE EVERYTHING WE CAN HUMANLY PERCEIVE, MAKES THE ASSEMBLAGE POINT JUMP OUTSIDE THE HUMAN DOMAIN AND PERCEIVE THE INCONCEIVABLE.*"
> —Carlos Castaneda, *from* The Art of Dreaming

Within the Tibetan Dzogchen tradition, lucid dreaming is considered a natural by-product of higher awareness or what the Tibetans call the practice of "natural light." Those who practice the Dzogchen system of dream yoga, however, take lucidity a step further, aiming to remain conscious as they slip into sleep, and then into the dream state. Given that scientific research shows that the first REM sleep begins about ninety minutes after a person falls asleep, it may seem implausible that these Eastern dreamworkers could be fully aware that they are sleeping.

"Yet," writes Patricia Garfield in *Creative Dreaming,* "it may well be fact. Yogi skills in body and thought control clearly surpass those of Western culture." The practices they use to promote lucid dreams include deep breathing and visualizing before going to sleep to relax the body and mind. These strategies, such as the one they call the "Practice of the Night," are said to "use the working of the mind in order eventually to go beyond the mind" and balance the "internal energies." According to Namkhai Norbu, one of the great Tibetan teachers, once the "energies" are "balanced," different kinds of "clarity dreams" will arise, such as dreams of future events or past lives. "Following the analogy of the sun, the clouds have now largely disappeared and the infinite rays of sunshine are able to manifest directly. . . . At that ultimate point dreams become awareness. . . . You use your practice so that your dreams influence daily life. This is the principal practice of the nighttime."

Here, step by step, are the essential elements of the "Practice of the Night," as described by Norbu in *Dream Yoga,* adapted for our readers' use to promote lucid dreaming. If you are interested, you might also wish to try entering "the state of natural light" that includes lucidity during sleep as well:

1. Relax the body—through baths, massage, and/or deep breathing. (Note: Paul Tholey suggests that, at this point, rather than mandate lucidity, you should give yourself the gentle suggestion that you will be conscious in your dream. If you like, he says, you can give yourself a specific action to perform in your dream that night, such as drinking a glass of water or tying your shoes—or perhaps Castaneda's idea of looking at your hands. The action can serve as a signal to you that you are dreaming.)

2. Concentrate on a white *A* at the center of your body that corresponds in the mind to the sound "ahh." (You can write the letter *A* on a piece of paper first, if you wish, and stare at it awhile to help yourself visualize it.)

3. Imagine a chain of *A*'s going up to the top of your head and then back down again. Repeat this until you fall asleep, with the *A* present in your mind. (If you have trouble falling asleep, just observe your thoughts and let them go.)

4. Enter into the state of dreams, in "the full presence of the state of natural light." (According to the Dzogchen tradition, the dreamer can actually remain aware of beginning to dream; Tibetans claim that if you exert your willpower, [lucidity] becomes familiar to you.)

5. Make the *A* sound immediately when you awaken and feel the presence of the white *A*. (According to Norbu, the Tibetan Dzogchen followers believe making the connection with the white *A* in the morning and again at night will enable the dreamer to "integrate into a state of contemplation or rigpa.")

6. Engage in this practice each night before going to sleep.

Combining ancient traditions with modern data on lucid dreams, we have devised a kind of "Practice of the Day," a few suggestions that may help you to develop the ability to have lucid dreams. According to the Tibetan tradition, it is the practices performed during waking hours that are the real dreamwork. The rest of the experience—while dreaming—"just happens," explains the Tibetan teacher Tenzin W. Rinpoche. But you must be diligent, Rinpoche adds, about doing the daily practices if you want to attain higher awareness while dreaming. Here are some things to try:

- ☾ If you have not yet mastered full awareness or lucidity in your dreams, attune yourself to your waking experiences with the same heightened awareness you hope to achieve in your dreams. "You should continually remind yourself," writes Norbu, "that all that you see and all that is done is none other than a dream." Tholey advises making a habit of asking yourself "Am I dreaming?" five to ten times a day, and again each time something unusual or dreamlike occurs (such as a helium balloon floating by, a rainfall cascading down on a sunny day, or anything else that seems improbable).

- ☾ Even after you achieve lucidity, you can use intense concentration on a particular theme or subject during the day to promote its appearance during the dream state.

- ☾ Try reliving a dream from the perspective of lucidity in order to promote lucid dreaming during sleep; this technique was proven successful by Gregory Scott Sparrow, a psychotherapist and the author of *Lucid Dreaming: Dreaming of the Clear Night*.

How will you know you're moving closer to lucid dreaming? Again, having an active relationship with your dreamworld will encourage more active dreaming: better recall, more vivid imagery, less fragmented images. It will also lead to more exploration of the dream environment while you are dreaming. You may not know you're dreaming, but you will begin to recognize people, places, and things that have appeared in other dreams, and you may ask yourself what one of these symbols means while in the dream. While learning to use dream language, one novice dreamworker had a dream with no apparent plot in which characters and objects appeared one after the other, each with some ostensibly symbolic meaning, in a somewhat disjointed fashion. As he was dreaming, he was aware that each had "meaning," though he was not sure what the meaning was. When a child who looked like neither boy nor girl appeared, and he said to himself in the dream, "This must represent the not-boy, not-girl part of me," he became frustrated and woke himself up—a typical prelucidity experience, and one that perhaps reflects his own difficulty feeling comfortable using dream language.

If possible, avoid waking yourself up; instead, move with the dream, following it where it leads. In time, you may begin to make choices and take actions within the dream. But remember, get the most out of this opportunity for active participation in the dream, you should take care not to dismiss or destroy any dream characters or objects prematurely. Allow yourself to remain in their presence, no matter how disturbing, in order to receive their message completely. Explore, rather than control. In time, and especially with practice, you can learn to welcome lucidity and to maintain it when it occurs.

Lucid dreaming has many uses—answering questions, resolving conflicts, and even helping to heal physical or psychological wounds. Perhaps people find success in this way because the dreaming mind is less threatened and more in control during the lucid dream state than during the waking state, and therefore more capable of confronting difficult issues. Further, the dreamer may have increased access to creative insight, healing effects, and problem-solving during a lucid dream. Whatever the reasons, lucid dreaming offers the serious dreamer a fertile ground in which to cultivate dream techniques while dreaming. One dreamer, who had suffered a serious physical assault while living in Moscow, used a recurring lucid dream to build back physical strength in her broken bones and muster up the emotional courage to move on with her life. Here are some excerpts from her dream commentary:

> *[In the dream,] I am lying in my bed in my apart-ment in Moscow, my knees piled high on four Russian pillows. I am aware of the limitations of my body and become afraid. I canvas the details of the room . . . and the black of night outside. I hear noise and picture a man climbing up the drainpipe outside. I actually see him through the lace curtains and the glass doors, climbing onto my balcony. He is the very large man who assaulted me, dressed in dark clothes and holding a gun. It is clear to me that he intends to shoot me, to finish his job.*

> *Then I direct it all: What options do I have in this dream? What can I do to protect myself? I slide across the sheets, and begin to roll to the left so that I can slide between my mattress and the wall. Only now I am stuck. I feel fear. If the man comes in, I have no place to go.*

> *So I tell myself to start the episode over.*

As she continues to have this dream, night after night during the first month of her recovery, this dreamer chooses to fortify herself in various ways against her intruder: In one dream, she has herself roll in a different direction, toward an exit. In another, she added more "props."

> *I started to see myself lying in bed with a particular nightgown, but this night I wore my body brace to*

bed so that I was stronger, first crawling and then over successive nights, finally getting up and running toward the living room to break a window (one night) and the front door (another night).

In reality, she says, she never wore the brace to bed, and was no stronger physically than she had been before. But in the dream, even as the danger increased, she was better equipped to deal with it, because her lucidity enabled her to prepare more and more each time she replayed the dream. She began to see this as a way of increasing her will to get well. Interestingly, even without knowing why she took a particular action (wearing her body brace, heading for the front door, and so on), she was still able to experience a feeling of growing emotional strength and healing.

GUIDED FANTASY

In lucid dreams, you are aware while you are dreaming. But can you dream while actually awake? Technically, no. But fantasy and daydreams have been defined as "a special case of imagery made up of a combination of memory and imagination images. . . . You could say that the images are part of an internal continuum, as in a film," according to Mike and Nancy Samuels, in their book *Seeing with the Mind's Eye*. Guided fantasy is just what it sounds like: A series of verbal or musical prompts guides your imagination through a scenario. The Samuels and others refer to this fantasy process as visualization; that is, creating a mental image or "picture in the mind."

Since the early day of hypnosis, psychologists, doctors, and yogis have used various visualization techniques to achieve specific goals. Doctors Joseph Breuer and Sigmund Freud were the first to systematically elicit images to treat patients, and psychiatrist Carl Jung used visualization extensively in his work, developing the

FIGURE 6.3: *Phyllis Koch-Sheras painted* Archetype, *after a guided fantasy about connecting with basic animal nature.*

technique of *active imagination* to bring forth archetypal images. More recently, behavior therapists such as Joseph Wolpe have used visualization techniques such as systematic desensitization to lessen anxiety, and Dr. Carl Simonton developed an effective visualization procedure for treating cancer. Other terms and techniques have evolved that are similar to guided fantasy: Hans Carl Leuner's guided affective imagery, Shakti Gawain's creative visualization, José Silva's mind control, and Robert Masters and Jean Houston's mind games, all use fantasy to expand consciousness.

Guided fantasy works well with a partner, but you can work solo as well, using a guided fantasy tape you purchase commercially or create yourself. Just like dreams, guided fantasy offers much material for interpretation; and almost any exercise you can do with a dream you can apply to guided fantasy also. Both dreams and guided fantasy are useful shortcuts to intuitive knowledge that is usually unconscious or ignored. Although fantasy is necessarily a more conscious experience than normal dreaming, you can still learn a lot about how your psyche responds to whatever images come up. Guided fantasy is a great place to begin dreamwork if you are a poor recaller or a non-recaller; your dreamworld may seem locked up tight, but you can always access your imagination.

In going through a guided fantasy, relaxation of both body and mind is key. Your goal is the alpha state you enter into just before sleep. Set the right mood, remove all distractions, and perhaps play some calming instrumental music. A sample guided fantasy is included here, originated by psychologist John Weir and reprinted from Phyllis Koch-Sheras's book *Dream On*. If you wish, tape-record it, complete with appropriate pauses, and then play it back when you are ready to complete the exercise. Where you see the ellipses, you should pause. Use it as is, or amend it to suit your own interest in pursuing this kind of "waking dream."

"Tree Fantasy"

It is a beautiful spring day. The sun is shining brightly and the breeze is blowing softly through the trees. You can hear the sounds of birds in the distance and smell the fragrance of flowers in the air.

Now, you realize that you are the seed of a tree being blown by the wind through the forest and across the fields. . . . You can feel yourself gently tossed through the air, preparing to find a place to settle into the earth. . . . Look around you, and see where you are being carried. . . . Now, the wind dies down and you notice where you have landed. . . . Gradually, you begin to feel yourself breaking out of your tight covering . . . sending down roots . . . now feel yourself pushing up, pushing up hard . . . harder . . . until finally you feel yourself breaking through the ground and rising up into the sunlight.

. . . Now feel your first leaves unfolding . . . feel yourself stretching and growing, making new leaves, and twigs, and branches, growing strong and tall . . . growing and growing . . . and growing. (Wait one to three minutes.) And now, I am going to count to three, and when I get to three, you will open your eyes and feel wide awake, remembering everything you have experienced, knowing you can use this information, now and in the future. One . . . start to come back . . . two . . . almost back . . . and three . . . open your eyes.

You can devise other symbolic experiences and narrate those on tape in a similar fashion: being born, traveling through your body, flying. You can use images and stories from your own dreams to create guided fantasies for yourself. You may want to consider guided fantasy as a prelude to dream incubation, which is the practice of consciously seeking out certain dreams and symbols. By making your imagination your friend, and inviting it to play an active role in your waking and sleeping lives, you open up a communication line between your conscious and unconscious minds. As you explore the meanings of your waking fantasy images, you can gain insight into the significance of these symbols as they appear in your dreams.

DREAM PLAY

All of these exercises are intended to be not only enlightening, but also fun to do. And it is in the spirit of fun that we encourage you to make your dreams your friends, to play with them and the messages they give you. If you experience a joyful or pleasant event in a dream, you might choose to recreate it in your waking life, inviting others to join you. (One woman dreamed she and her friends were eating a giant burrito in her kitchen, which gave her the idea for a giant burrito party.) If a certain image recurs in your dreams (an elephant, a banana, a rainbow), you might begin acquiring items that feature that image. Dream incubation is not only useful, but entertaining. So use the technique to invite yourself to have fun in your dreams.

Dreamwork 2000: High-Tech Options for Dreamers

A burgeoning interest in dreams has led to several innovations for dreamers. Here are a few highlights, with contact numbers for those who wish to know more:

NovaDreamer, designed by lucid dreaming expert Stephen LaBerge, Ph.D., is designed for those who want to learn to lucid dream. This apparatus looks like a space alien's headpiece, and is intended to alert sleepers to periods of REM sleep with light or sound signals (you choose). These cues will not fully awaken you, but they will cue you in that you're dreaming, giving you the chance to participate more actively in guiding your dreams. For $275, dreamers receive a package that includes a course in lucid dreaming, a one-year membership in the Lucidity Institute, and a subscription to a quarterly newsletter. Available through Mind Gear, 1-800-525-MIND.

Dreamwork by mail. Need help interpreting a dream? Dream researcher Robert Van de Castle, author of *Our Dreaming Mind,* offers consultation by mail; the cost is $50 for a half-hour audiotaped response to your written dreams. For a brochure on this service, write Dreams, P.O. Box 3048, University Station, Charlottesville, VA 22903.

Dreamwork on-line. Tapping into a discussion group on-line allows you to communicate with dreamworkers from all over the country. Use one of the data base searching sites to find user's groups that are discussing dreams.

A dream workout. "Henry Reed's Dream Interpretation Workout" is a videotape designed by a well-known dream consultant to bring dreamwork right to your television screen. The video costs $49.95 and is available through Video Home Companion, P.O. Box 1541, Virginia Beach, VA 23451.

Why not incubate a dream in which you travel to your favorite places, or make love to your favorite person, or perform some amazing acts?

The dream play approach can find its way into many different activities, and it is easy to incorporate into any of the exercises in this chapter. If you think about it, dreamwork isn't all work—there is also a great deal of fun involved. And if a dream symbol leaves you feeling really good, why not incorporate it somehow into your waking life? Bake a dream cake! Design a dream T-shirt! Whatever you do, thank your dream for giving you this gift. You may find that the result is a richer, more rewarding dream life, with better recall and that much more to work and play with each morning of your waking life. Chapter 7 offers more ways to "sleep on it," presenting techniques for enhancing your creativity through dreamwork.

CHAPTER SEVEN

SLEEPING ON IT
USING DREAMS
TO ENHANCE YOUR
CREATIVITY, PRODUCTIVITY,
AND HEALING

What do golf champion Jack Nicklaus, best-selling author Anne Rice, and scientific genius Albert Einstein have in common? What about nineteenth-century English poet Samuel Taylor Coleridge, pop entertainer Steve Allen, and surrealist painter Salvador Dali? Despite diverse interests and areas of expertise, all of these notable achievers share an interesting point of inspiration: dreams.

Creativity is the source of great works of literature, music, and art. But it is also the driving force behind such things as decision making, scientific innovation, and entrepreneurship. All of us are creative. How do we know for sure? Because all of us dream. Dream thought is similar to creative thought: Unlike logical deduction, dream thought uses a single image as a jumping-off point, following not where logic might guide, but whatever cross-references the dreamer makes, building image upon image until the scenario is complete. The dreaming mind is free of inhibition, free of the fear of judgment. You might think of dreaming as brainstorming: Through free association, word play, symbolism, and perhaps some random image making, the dreaming mind exercises the creative skills even as the waking mind sleeps.

Most creative thinkers agree that letting an idea gel is an important part of the creative process. You are probably familiar with this stage of creativity. You have considered all the angles, gathered information, explored possibilities. Now, you're ready just to sit with the problem for a while and let it incubate. Then, when you least expect it, a new idea emerges fully formed. If you're like many people, you might "sleep on it," waking up in the morning with a fresh perspective and a clear new direction.

Usually, this type of problem-solving occurs randomly—a person goes to bed, dreams about a problem, and then wakes up knowing just what to do. But there are also techniques for dream incubation—the act of asking your dreaming mind to come up with an idea or solve a problem while you are sleeping. In chapter 6, we look at some of the ways that creating art can enhance your understanding of dreams. In

> "*I CAN NEVER DECIDE WHETHER MY DREAMS ARE THE RESULT OF MY THOUGHTS OR MY THOUGHTS ARE THE RESULT OF MY DREAMS.*"
> —*D. H. Lawrence, English writer*

this chapter, we explore the other side of the equation: how dreams, whether random or induced, can enhance your artistic creations.

A good place to begin learning about dreams and creativity is a survey of the dreams of some creative people. As you read about their dream-inspired achievements, keep in mind that you need not be an artist, scientist, or scholar to derive great benefit from creative dreaming. Asking your dreams to assist you can help you design an addition to your house, improve your jump shot, landscape your garden, allocate human resources at your company, plan a family vacation, or improve relationships with your friends and family.

DREAM-INSPIRED LITERATURE

The earliest Greek plays are said to have come from dream stories. And many of the great works of Western literature had their impetus in dreams. Theodor Dostoyevsky, Voltaire, James Joyce, and many other classic authors turned to their dreamworlds for creative energy. Even today, contemporary authors look to their dreamworlds for characters, stories, and even a solution to the dreaded writer's block. In Naomi Epel's book *Writers Dreaming*, Anne Rivers Siddons, the popular author of such novels as *Peachtree Road, Outer Banks,* and *Colony,* comments: "I think every creative impulse that a working writer, or artist of any sort, has comes out of that dark old country where dreams come from."

The nineteenth-century English poet William Blake is known as much for his elaborate illustrations as for his verse. Not only were his literary and artistic creations said to have come from dreams and what he called "visions," but he also devised a new and more cost-effective means of printing his works after having a dream that led him to switch to copper printing plates. Samuel Taylor Coleridge wrote his evocative poem *Kubla Khan* based on an exceptionally vivid dream in which he claims to have "heard" all of the two hundred-plus lines. The poem's unusual imagery is distinctly dream- like: "In Xanadu did Kubla Khan/A stately pleasure dome decree:/Where Alph, the sacred river, ran/Through caverns measureless to man/Down to a sunless sea." Like modern dreamworkers, Coleridge is said to have scribbled down everything he could remember immediately upon waking; unfortunately, so the story goes, his maid knocked on the door, interrupting his train of thought and causing him to lose the last verse. Robert Louis Stevenson relied on the "little people" or "Brownies" he said were responsible for giving him the stories that took place in his dreams, turning to them deliberately in search of

> "*I SHOULD HAVE LOST MANY A GOOD HIT, HAD I NOT SET DOWN AT ONCE THINGS THAT OCCURRED TO ME IN MY DREAMS.*"
> —*Sir Walter Scott, Scottish author*

inspiration for his fiction. *The Strange Case of Dr. Jekyll and Mr. Hyde* was one such gift. And Mary Shelley was a young woman of only twenty when she wrote *Frankenstein; or, The Modern Prometheus,* a book whose main character, a laboratory experiment that becomes a manmade monster, first appeared to her in a dream.

In the United States, Edgar Allen Poe's eerie stories are known for their otherworldly surrealism. His short story "The Lady Ligeia" is one of several that were inspired by an image first seen in a dream, in this case her haunting eyes. More recently, Anne Rice, author of the acclaimed series of vampire novels beginning with *The Queen of the Damned* and including *Interview with the Vampire,* which became a feature film in 1994, pulls dream images into her waking life in order to create the hauntingly memorable characters that populate her novels. And Amy Tan, the Chinese-American author of *The Joy Luck Club* and *The Kitchen God's Wife,* has relied on dreams for personal guidance as well as literary inspiration. She takes creative dreaming one step further, by actively seeking solutions to her writing quandaries. In *Writers Dreaming,* she remarks, "Sometimes, if I'm stuck on the ending of a story, I'll just take the story with me to bed. I'll let it become part of a dream and see if something surfaces. . . . I don't normally see my characters in dreams exactly as they appear in a book, but I do experience a similar kind of feeling or emotion, something that gives me new insight into the questions that I'm asking of those characters."

DREAM-INSPIRED ART

The surrealists of the early twentieth century are probably most closely associated with dream imagery in painting. Anyone who has seen a painting such as Salvadore Dali's *Persistence of Memory* no doubt recalls the impossible, yet realistic, quality of the melting clocks that dot the can-vas. "Am I dreaming?"—the ques-tion lucid dreamers often ask themselves—seems especially appro-priate when confronting a surrealist work: Surrealists rely on images that appear realistic, `drawn or painted in perspective, with appropriate color and shading. But the scenarios depicted are bizarre and fanciful, much like the content of a dream. In fact, the surrealists took Sigmund Freud's *The Interpretation of Dreams* as a kind of call to action, and made it their mission to use his technique of free association to create a genre of psychoanalytic painting intended to tap the uncon-scious. Dali himself acknowledged the large debt he owed to his dreams, calling his paintings "hand-painted dream pho-tographs." Other types of artists, too, have relied on dreams to provide imagery and insights, symbols and solutions, using such techniques as lucid dreaming and dream incubation.

> *"IF THE DREAM IS A TRANSLATION OF WAKING LIFE, WAKING LIFE IS ALSO A TRANSLATION OF THE DREAM."*
> —René Magritte, Belgian surrealist painter

DREAM-INSPIRED MUSIC

Ancient cultures looked to dreams to inspire their music and rit-ual songs. Indeed, many dreamers of today hear songs in their dreams, and some find it quite revealing to uncover the message their lyrics contain. Pop musicians such as Paul McCartney, Billy Joel, and Stevie Nicks have all looked to dreams to add a creative dimension to their work. Classical musicians, too, have drawn from their dream music to create musical masterpieces. Richard Wagner attributed the opera *Tristan und Isolde* to a dream. And *The Messiah,* a breathtaking holiday favorite, is based in part on music composer George Frideric Handel first "heard" in a dream. And in 1954, Steve Allen dreamed some of the lyrics of what was to become "This Could Be the Start of Something Big," which was one of his greatest successes.

DREAM-INSPIRED SCIENTIFIC DISCOVERY

To the uninitiated, science might seem to be anything but a creative endeavor. But consider: In science, as in art, a person gathers information, materials, or facts and then responds to them in a new way, taking what is known and making something new from it, which is the essence of creativity. Like artists, scientists go to sleep at night with thoughts and ideas swirling in their heads, awaiting the inspiration that will make sense from seeming nonsense. Indeed, many inventions and discoveries have come from the stuff of dreams.

> "*IN DREAMS WE CATCH GLIMPSES OF A LIFE LARGER THAN OUR OWN. . . . THOUGHTS ARE IMPARTED TO US FAR ABOVE OUR ORDINARY THINKING.*"
> —*Helen Keller, blind–deaf author and educator*

Inventor Elias Howe toiled unsuccessfully for years before a scary dream led to the invention of the sewing machine in the mid-nineteenth century. The problem was the needle. The solution? In his dream, Howe was captured by savages whose leader commanded him to complete his invention. As he looked around at the warriors in the crowd, he saw that their spearheads were punctured with eye-shaped holes. Unlike sewing needles, which featured a point on one end and an eye for thread on the other, Howe's sewing machine needle was unique. And it worked!

Scientists have puzzled through many a difficult riddle in their sleep. In 1890, German chemist Friedrich Kekulé von Stradonitz figured out the carbon-ring structure of the benzene molecule after a dream in which a snake touching head to tail pointed him in the right direction. Niels Bohr's dream of planets encircling the sun inspired him to theorize that electrons revolve around atoms. A dream resulted in a 1903 Nobel Prize for Otto Loewi, who came up with an experiment that proved nerve impulses were transmitted not electrically but chemically; according to author Ann Faraday, however, Loewi actually experienced cryptomnesia, or "forgotten memory," having actually hypothesized the same theory eighteen years earlier and then forgetting it. Albert Einstein's famous theory of relativity— $E=MC^2$—also has its origins in a dream.

DREAM-INSPIRED ATHLETICS

A favorite story dreamworkers like to repeat is how professional golfer Jack Nicklaus used a dream to get out of a slump. Despite intensive training, he continued to play badly. A dream in which he used a new grip changed his luck, however. The next time he played, he tried holding his club as he had in the dream, and his playing improved. Other athletes, too, have found guidance in dreams. German psychologist Paul Tholey, a lucid dreaming expert and skateboard champion, has used dreamwork to improve his own and others' athletic performance, building on a common sports psychology technique called mental imaging, a visualization strategy that enhances performance. (Athletes such as skier Jean-Claude Killy and tennis player Chris Evert have used mental imaging to improve their performances.) According to the book *Control Your Dreams,* Tholey's theory is that "the amount of actual practice time can be dramatically reduced by rehearsals that recreate the whole athletic environment while [lucid] dreaming"—that is, the roar of the crowd, the feel of the terrain, the intensity of the competition, all of which are perhaps best simulated by the dreaming mind. Sports psychology is a rapidly growing field, and it is to be expected that, along with visualization and other kinds of waking fantasy, work with dreams will find a prominent place among the techniques an athlete relies on for sports success.

YOUR CREATIVITY AND DREAMS

The relation between the dream state and the waking state of creativity is a direct one. And the achievements of creative dreamers are not limited to the fine or performing arts. Indeed, any original idea is a creative one. Anything imagined can take its inspiration from a dream—not just artistic creations, but decisions of any kind. You can draw on your dream experiences to solve problems at work, in your relationships, and at home with your family. You can use your dreams to help heal yourself and encourage personal growth in some very direct ways.

"But I'm not a creative person," you may say. Everyone is. Everyone dreams. Of course, creativity is not automatic—whether you are dreaming or awake. But abandoning the negative thoughts that block your creativity and then learning to call up that creativity through dreamwork will enable you to access your creativity immediately, whenever you like. Don't give in to creator's block. Instead, trust your creative self and enlist your dreams to open up your creativity.

DREAM INCUBATION: THE TECHNIQUE

Most creative dreams occur spontaneously, born of whatever currently preoccupies the mind in waking life. But it is possible,

and even more produc-
tive, to use dreamwork
techniques to actively
incubate creative dreams.
Prompting your dreams to
help you answer ques-
tions, solve problems, or
see new variations on a
familiar theme transforms
the dream experience.
Dream incubation may
sound like a tall order but,
in fact, with practice, you
will get results. Along the
way, pay special attention
to the contents of your
dreams; you will probably
begin to see some rele-
vance to the questions you
are presenting. Eventually,

> "THE LANGUAGE OF STORYTELLING
> AND POETRY IS THE POWERFUL
> SISTER OF THE DREAM LANGUAGE.
> FROM THE ANALYSIS OF MANY
> DREAMS (BOTH CONTEMPORARY
> AND ANCIENT ONES TAKEN FROM
> WRITTEN ACCOUNTS) OVER THE
> YEARS, AS WELL AS SACRED TEXTS
> AND THE WORKS OF MYSTICS SUCH
> AS CATHERINE OF SIENA, FRANCIS
> OF ASSISI, RUMI, AND ECKHART
> AND THE WORK OF MANY POETS
> SUCH AS DICKINSON, MALLAY,
> WHITMAN, AND SO ON, THERE
> APPEARS TO BE WITHIN THE PSYCHE
> A POETRY MAKING AND ART MAKING
> FUNCTION THAT ARISES WHEN A
> PERSON SPONTANEOUSLY OR
> PURPOSELY VENTURES NEAR THE
> INSTINCTIVE CORE OF THE PSYCHE."
> —Clarissa Pinkola Estés, Ph.D.,
> from Women Who Run
> With the Wolves.

you will be able to make productive use of the dreaming mind's
natural tendency to focus on whatever your waking mind is
concerned with.

Building on the dreamwork exercises of chapter 6—especially
Creating a Special Dream Space on page 149—we offer the following dream incubation strategies. No matter which technique,
or combination of techniques, you employ, it is essential that you
remain open to the possibility of your creativity emerging
through your dreams.

Think about it: Determine what problem or question you
want to work on, then think about it in depth. What is your
goal? What has gotten in the way, or is an obstacle now? What

do you know about the problem? What things seem impossible to know for sure? Now, settle on a single question that sums up your concerns. Be specific, and try again if you don't get an answer; sometimes rephrasing the question is the jump start your dreaming mind needs to provide you with a solution.

Put it in writing: Identify an area you would like to work on—a question you want to ask, a dilemma you are facing, or a direction you may pursue. Formulate a question, then concentrate on it for a few minutes just before bedtime. Write the question down in your dream journal or on a slip of paper and put it under your pillow. As you go to sleep, repeat the question in your mind.

Use creative meditation: This exercise draws on Carl Jung's concept of a collective unconscious, turning to the creativity inherent in all of us for inspiration and power. Before you begin, take a few minutes to relax and focus on the moment. Then, repeat the following statements. You may wish to modify them somewhat or speak them aloud, or perhaps commit them to memory. (If you prefer, you can write them down in your dream journal.)

I know that I am an integral part of the universe.

My consciousness is intimately connected with the consciousness of all things.

This fantastic pool of consciousness and creativity is available to me whenever I wish to experience it. Tonight, as I dream, I will immerse myself in this boundless pool of creativity, adding what I can and drawing from it what I need most.

Tomorrow I will awaken a better person for it. As always, I promise to make the most of any dreams I remember when I awaken.

Now allow yourself to fall asleep, remaining open to all creative possibilities.

Remember, successful dream incubation takes practice, and there is often a lot of trial and error as a dreamer learns to use this remarkable technique. Joan Windsor, author of *Healing & Dreams: Expanding the Inner Eye*, suggests sleeping later than usual one morning a week, which she says "will provide an additional opportunity for a broader spectrum of spiritual insights to be previewed by the dreaming mind." Continue with the dream-work exercises we discuss in other chapters, and pay careful attention to the messages your dreams contain. In these messages, you may find the answers you are looking for, even if they do not at first glance seem to be direct responses to your incubating questions. The next sections offer a closer look at using both spontaneous and incubated dreams to enhance your creativity, productivity, and healing capability.

YOUR CREATIVE DREAMS

Amateur and professional artists alike can use dreams to enhance their work both in direct ways, such as recreating on the canvas some actual imagery from a dream, and in indirect ways, such as applying a dream message to a project. A novelist who was struggling to achieve richness with her characters decided to incubate a dream that would tell her what to do next. That night, she dreamed about a crooked house—crooked staircase, crooked railing, crooked walls and floors. Upon waking she realized that what her novel needed was characters with a little crookedness! A part of her knew her characters were all too "nice," but it took a dream to make it clear to her.

A graphic designer was charged with the task of creating a logo for a local crafts fair, but could not seem to get it right, despite numerous tries and several discussions with her client. Asking her dreams to help her, the artist dreamed very literally about her problem:

"The Logo"
I am working on my sketches. I begin work on a new idea. I draw two hands carving a rabbit out of wood. To emphasize the impression of the rabbit as something only beginning to come into being, I draw the artist's hands in great detail to contrast with the broad lines and unfinished surfaces of the rabbit.

Immediately after waking up, the artist repeated in waking life what she had done in her dreams, creating a logo that was exactly what she wanted—the logo of her dreams!

To use your own dreams to create art, literature, music, dance, or other inspired results, try these tips:

◖ After each dream, note any particularly vivid dream images, words, or feelings. You may wish to use them later in a drawing, painting, dance, story, play, or novel. They may even provide material for a slogan, logo, or joke.

◖ Use dream interpretation techniques to determine the extent to which your dream symbols reflect creative parts of yourself.

◖ Examine your dreams for any relation to the creative process. What are you working on now? How does your dream suggest a way around it? Sometimes a dream offers a comment on your creative self as a whole, rather than on the project you are currently working on. For example, a songwriter who lacked confidence in her singing voice had a dream in which she sang out in a strong, beautiful voice; the dream seemed to suggest to her that vocalizing with more confidence would improve her sound.

◖ And finally, use dream incubation techniques to ask specific questions about your work, or to seek inspiration on a new direction to follow, or even a new medium to try. Always be specific, because dreams tend to answer the precise question you ask them.

YOUR PRODUCTIVITY AND DREAMS

Creativity finds its way into our decision-making processes every day, as we weigh our options, imagining different scenarios, and then selecting the action we believe will bring us what we want. On the job, in volunteer committees, within the family, brainstorming is a daily occurrence. Why not do some of your brainstorming during the 20 percent of your life you spend sleeping? As history shows, the results can be powerful.

If you have ever tapped your dreamworld to enhance your working productivity, you are not alone. For example, computer genius Alan Huang found what he needed in a recurring dream that led to a major breakthrough. According to *Success* magazine, Huang's dream featured two battalions of sorcerers who marched steadily toward each other, pails of data in hand. After dreaming that these armies were able to move right through each other, Huang saw the light: In order to create the optical computer he was striving for, he would need to utilize currents that could intersect. In time, he developed a laser computer model.

According to creativity expert Charles "Chic" Thompson,

who himself uses dreams for creative problem-solving, research shows that "while falling asleep or waking up" is the fifth-best "idea-friendly" time; "after waking up in the middle of the night" ranks eighth. Thompson, who has consulted for such major corporations as General Electric and NASA, discusses creative dreaming in his book *What a Great Idea!* "A dream is our moment of pure creativity," he says. "It's like five hundred ideas all Scotch-taped together." Thompson has these suggestions for collecting your "dreamed-up ideas":

◖ Use dream interpretation techniques to remember and document your dreams.

◖ Free-associate during your hypnagogic and hypnomonic dreams—the falling-asleep and waking-up stages of sleep. After you awaken, continue to lie still, eyes closed, and see where your mind takes you.

◖ Write down as many dream ideas as you can recall. "Do not be discouraged if some of your ideas do not make any sense," writes Thompson. "Remember, you're after large quantities of ideas. Just throw the bad ones away."

Dream incubation is a particularly useful problem-solving technique. To incubate a solution to something that has been on your mind, follow this procedure:

◖ Gather as much information as possible, and spend some time thinking about it before you go to sleep.

◖ Just before bed, narrow your question down as much as possible, then focus on it in one of the

ways we describe in the section Dream
Incubation: The Technique. Be specific. For
example, asking your dreams "What would
change the way I interact with my boss?" is more
precise than "How can I do better at work?"

YOUR HEALING AND DREAMS

We have talked before about personal health as a common
dream theme. Because our minds take in so much information
every day, far more than we are consciously aware of, we are
often more in sync with our bodies than we think. Subliminal
perceptions, the bits of information our unconscious takes in,
appear from many different sources: news reports we watch,
articles we read, conversations we overhear, our physical feelings
and experiences, advertisements we see. Everything we take in
has the potential to speak back to us in a dream, sometimes
offering a new perspective on our physical health. You need not
be ill to have a dream point the way to better health. For example, a woman with a slight vitamin deficiency had ignored this
health concern until she had the following dream:

"The Iron C"
I'm looking at my naked body from outside of
myself. A zipper appears in my belly and unzips. An
object comes out of my body that is shaped like the
letter C and made of iron. It disappears inside my
body and the zipper closes.

After this dream, the woman decided to increase her intake of
these nutrients, which she says she "never seemed to get enough
of." You don't need to wait idly for a healing dream to happen
to you. You can make it happen. Dream incubation allows you
to prompt your dreams to offer you advice and guidance about
your physical health.

Healing dreams are also dreams that promote strength and recovery. (The lucid dreams of the woman recovering from a physical assault in Russia are a good example of using dreams creatively for healing; you may recall how, each time she dreamed, she bolstered herself up for increased strength, symbolizing her growing emotional strength and her physical healing.) A leukemia patient has found that the symbols in her dreams have a healing effect. From the beginning of her diagnosis, she had had dreams about hunting the wolf that for her represented her cancer. Here is an excerpt from her journal:

> *The horse and I are hunting the wolf. It is a very dark, moonless night and the wolf is a milky blur, streaking over the rolling grasslands of the steppe with us in hot pursuit. Running toward us is a huge herd of animals. At first I don't recognize them. Then as they get closer, I realize it is a huge pack of wolfhounds, hundreds of animals strong. The wolf veers off but they overtake it easily and it disappears under a boiling mass of snarling bodies. The horse and I stop a respectful distance away. A minute or two later all that is left are a few bloody tufts of white fur in the trampled grass.*

This dreamer awoke in excrutiating pain, a reminder, she writes, of "how hard my marrow is working to regenerate itself. This dream makes an interesting testimonial to the resurgence of my white blood cells. I look forward to the day when I go up there and find the wolf, and the leukemia it represents, already dead." The powerful imagery of this dream reflects the dreamer's physical battle with her illness, presenting the physical process as a story she can understand and participate in. Psychological healing, too, is possible in dreams. For example, an elderly woman whose husband died not long ago finds comfort in the dreams she has in which he holds her tenderly. No dreamwork has to take place for the healing to begin. Sometimes, merely having the dream experience is enough to effect change.

Herbal Dream Blends

For centuries, herbal remedies have helped heal the sick. But they are also used to stimulate brain activity such as creative thinking and even better dreaming.

Earthwares, an herb shop in Carmel, California, offers Dream Tea, an herbal tea intended to help "nondreamers" remember the many dreams they have each night, and to cause dreamers to recall their dreams more vividly.

The tea is an equal blend of the following herbs: mugwort, a Native American and generally well-known dream amplifier; rosemary; kava kava, a Polynesian herb used in preparation for vision quests; lemon grass; red raspberry leaf; alfalfa; and spearmint.

Contact an herbalist or natural foods store to obtain the concoction, or get in touch with Judith Bean, proprietor of Earthwares, 122 Crossroads, Carmel, CA 93923, 1-800-455-HERB; the tea costs two dollars an ounce.

If you are interested in "sleeping on it," you might try a dream pillow filled with herbs that are said to encourage dream recall and induce clarity in the dream state. A combination of the legendary mugwort and lavender, rose petals, white sage, yerba santa, and lilac flowers is the mix preferred by Native Scents in Taos, New Mexico, which markets sachet-sized dream pillows. If you like, you can buy these herbs yourself and mix them into the stuffing of your own favorite pillow. Sweet dreams!

Relationships are seen in a new light. Actions and injustices are rectified or made clearer. A dream experience can resonate in much the same way as a waking one, and provide insight, healing, and, finally, closure.

INCUBATING A HEALING DREAM

To incubate a healing dream regarding your general health, concentrate on your physical body as you fall asleep, focusing on your overall well-being. Give yourself the suggestion that you will dream about a way to improve your well-being. When you wake up, follow your usual dream interpretation practice. When you have a specific health concern, state your "request" as concisely as possible (for example, "What is causing my backache?"). Your dreams will listen very carefully, giving you the answer to the exact question you asked. If you do not get results with one question, try phrasing it a different way.

It is also possible to have a healing dream about another person. This is not surprising, because family and friends often appear in the dreamworld, representing parts of ourselves or perhaps themselves as they appear to be. When someone we care about is taken ill in a dream, the emotions that arise can be unsettling. Given everything our waking minds take in, it is certainly possible to have a healing dream about someone else: Perhaps we have observed symptoms characteristic of a particular condition, or heard the person talk about feeling under the weather. The question is, When is a dream about someone else's health condition worth sharing, and when should we simply do our dreamwork and keep the dream to ourselves? Here are some simple guidelines to help you make that decision:

C First, interpret the dream from your own perspective, using dream language to connect with each character as a part of yourself. What aspects of you does this person represent? What might the health condition signify in your own life?

◖ Next, consider the character as him- or herself, with the condition in question. Could the scenario be symbolic of something currently happening in your waking life? You might then choose to share the dream with the other person, using it as a starting point for discussion. For example, a woman who was going through a difficult period in her marriage dreamed her husband had cancer. Using dream interpretation techniques, she discovered that the cancer was a metaphor for what was eating away at her marriage. Rather than rush her husband off to the oncologist, she chose to talk about her concerns, and the couple gained new understanding of their relationship. (Even when the condition is symbolic, however, there may be some health-related symptom worth looking into, so do not discount your dreaming intuition.)

◖ Finally, think about the other person's current health status, and what bearing the dream might in fact have. Generally, there is no great risk in sharing a healing dream with another; take care, however, not to scare someone with a dire diagnosis that may turn out to be a mere metaphor for something else entirely. In the end, the decision is yours to make. Perhaps you want to consider whether recounting the dream will offer real assistance and the possibility of a cure.

You can also try incubating a dream to help another person. If you like, you might ask to borrow a personal item that will help you focus on the person. You can then take it to bed with you, concentrating on it as you give yourself the suggestion that you will dream for your friend's benefit. Often, the dream will not seem relevant to you, only to become crystal clear when you share it with the person you dreamed it for, who may have a better knowledge of his or her own circumstances and health.

A FINAL WORD

If you have tried the dreamwork exercises in chapter 6, you realize how many creative possibilities exist in dreams even for dreamers who call themselves noncreative. People who have never before drawn a picture, written a poem, or developed a fictional character find themselves captivated by the images, words, and people in their dreams, all of which are creations of their own dreaming minds. As you become fluent in your own personal dream language, you will get to know your creative side. In time, you will find yourself turning to that part of yourself for ideas and innovations in many aspects of your life. When a creative inspiration enters your consciousness through a dream, welcome it as the long-lost child of your dreaming mind, and take what it has to offer you.

"Creativity and dreaming are inextricably intertwined," writes psychoanalyst Jill Morris, author of *The Dream Workbook*. "They are both functions of the right brain, using the same well of memory, wisdom, and personal symbolism, and they both spring from the unconscious. In dreams, the raw feelings are thrown up in haphazard, symbolic form. In a creative endeavor, the same material is consciously transformed, through the disciplines of the particular medium and the creator's individual sensibilities, into a work of art." You might think of your dreaming mind as yourself unedited. In creating your dreams, you don't stop to think about what is logical, appropriate, moral, ethical, or even desirable. You simply *experience*—following dream life wherever it leads. Creativity at its best is an uninhibited effort, a boundless explosion of ideas and insights that only you can ignite. When you want to enhance your creativity, dreams are a fine place to start and an excellent place to come back to. Sometimes, the creativity of dreams has an aura of the supernatural, so accurately do dreams predict the future or communicate with fellow dreamers. In the next chapter, we explore psychic phenomena and dreams.

CHAPTER EIGHT

COINCIDENCE? MAYBE
PSYCHIC PHENOMENA AND DREAMS

It is 1865. Abraham Lincoln, the sixteenth president of the United States, is asleep in the White House. Entering a state of REM sleep, he begins to dream. At first, he hears people sobbing. Following the sound, he wanders down the stairs in search of its source. His eyes land upon a coffin, but he is unable to see the face of the deceased. Turning to a nearby soldier, he inquires about the deceased. "It is the President," the soldier responds, "killed by an assassin."

A few days later, Abraham Lincoln was murdered.

It is 1912. The *Titanic*, an immense passenger ship, is making its way from England to New York. On land, a young girl dreams she is walking along a road near her home when she suddenly spies a massive sinking ship. She hears a scream, and awakens; when she falls back to sleep, she has the same nightmare. Elsewhere, a man who has booked passage on the *Titanic* dreams more than once that he sees the ship floating askew, with people scrambling about in the surrounding sea; a change in plans prevents his getting aboard.

A few days after these dreams, the *Titanic* sinks, killing 1,500 people.

As a young soldier, Adolph Hitler dreamed of being buried alive by dirt and iron, with blood running from his chest. When he awoke, he felt a strong urge to leave the trench he was sleeping in. Not long after he escaped, a shell exploded where he had lain, killing everyone who remained.

Rational science has yet to explain paranormal dreams—dreams such as these that contain knowledge of events that have not yet occurred or are as yet unknown to the waking mind. But thousands of such dreams have been documented both anecdotally and in laboratory studies by such notable researchers as Ian Stephenson at the University of Virginia and Drs. J. B. and Louisa Rhine of the Duke University Parapsychology Laboratory. Scientists use the Greek letter *psi* to refer to paranormal occurrences such as extrasensory perception (ESP), mind over matter (psychokinesis), and mental telepathy. And while little is known about how and why psi dreams take place, there is much research documenting their occurrence. For some dreamers, a psi dream is an isolated event, occurring just once in their lives; others experience psi dreams more frequently. Women report more psi dreams than men, and death and accidents are the most common subject matter.

UNDERSTANDING PARANORMAL OR PSI DREAMS

How can our dreaming mind know things that our waking mind cannot? We discuss some possibilities in the previous chapter. Information enters our mind through numerous channels: what

we read, what people tell us, what we observe, what we overhear. In some ways, the mind is like a radio, with the dial tuned
to one station, which comes in loud and clear, while the other
stations continue broad-
casting. If a part of our
minds is able to tune in
to these other frequen-
cies, then perhaps psi
dreaming becomes possi-
ble. Science has yet to
solve this mystery. But, as Montague Ullman and Nan
Zimmerman write in *Working with Dreams,* "The existence of
these phenomena suggests that while asleep, we are not only able
to scan backward in time and tap into our remote memory, but
are also able to scan forward in time and across space to tap into
information outside our own experience." There are four types
of psi dreams: precognitive, clairvoyant, telepathic, and mutual.

> "*MEN HAVE CONCEIVED A
> TWOFOLD USE OF SLEEP: THAT IT IS
> A REFRESHING OF THE BODY IN
> THIS LIFE; THAT IT IS A PREPARING
> OF THE SOUL FOR THE NEXT.*"
> —*John Donne, English poet*

Precognitive dreams: A precognitive dream depicts an event
that later happens. You dream that your tire goes flat, then sure
enough, within days, you have a flat tire. You dream that someone dies, and before you know it, the sad news arrives. Lincoln
and Hitler apparently experienced precognitive dreams, as did
those who had dream premonitions about the sinking of the
Titanic. Although sometimes hard to verify, these dreams do
occur, often in people who do not otherwise experience ESP. We
know of one man who has had several precognitive dreams
about the death of those close to him: In one instance, he
dreamed his cousin would die in a motorcycle crash; within
days, it happened. Another night as he lay sleeping next to the
woman he lived with, he dreamed his great-aunt died, and
awoke from the dream with a start; within hours, a call came in
and he discovered it was not his great-aunt, but his girlfriend's

grandmother who had died—at the exact time he had been having the dream!

Clairvoyant dreams: In a clairvoyant or, to translate from
the French, "clear-seeing" dream, the dreamer sees an event or
object that truly exists in waking life without any foreknowledge
of it whatsoever. No one has described it to the dreamer, no one
has shown the dreamer a picture of it. Yet the person, place, or
thing turns out to be precisely the same as it appeared in the
dream. People use another French expression, déjà vu, meaning
"already seen," to describe the feeling of having been somewhere or done something before; a clairvoyant dream carries
with it a distinct sense of déjà vu. One woman we talked to, for
example, reported a feeling of déjà vu that she recognized as
dream fragments that were recurring during her waking life—a
person reaching for a glass, a police car moving into the traffic
lane in front of her, and so forth.

Sometimes, a clairvoyant dream seems to allow the dreamer
to view faraway events as they are taking place. A man we interviewed reported the following clairvoyant experience: "In a
dream, I am watching my brother and a friend drive down a
winding country road at night in a Japanese compact car—I
thought it was a Toyota. The dream seemed really vivid and real,
so much so that I woke up and decided I had to call my brother."
Just then, the telephone in the dreamer's hotel room rang—but it
was after midnight, and no one but his parents knew where he
had gone on vacation. To this dreamer's surprise, it was his
brother. "It was the weirdest thing," the dreamer recalls. "My
brother said, 'I know you'll think this is strange, but I believe I
saw you crossing the road tonight.' " A chill went up his spine
and the dreamer responded, "Was it a winding road? Were you
in a small Japanese car?" The brother answered yes. "It was
eerie," the dreamer recalls. "The only thing different was that

the car was a Nissan." He laughs. "But I never could tell those two types of cars apart."

Telepathic dreams: In a telepathic dream, direct communication takes place between the dreamer and another person. You dream that your cousin tells you she is pregnant, and a day or two later, she calls with the happy news. The following example appears to contain a telepathic message:

> *"Warning"*
> *I run into David, my former boyfriend. He is glad to see me. "It's been a long time," he says. "Yes, it has been." I tell him I want to talk to him, but I will have to come back later.*

Within minutes of awakening, this dreamer heard a doorbell ring. It was David, come to discuss a reconciliation after several months without contact. The dreamer had no inkling he might be on his way over. Fortunately, she says, the dream prepared her for this surprise. "I wisely took my dream's advice," she recalls, "and told him I wanted to talk to him, but needed some time to think things over first."

Mutual dreams: Mutual dreams occur when two or more people dream strikingly similar dreams on the same night. Often cultivated in dream laboratories and workshops, these dreams are frequently offered as proof that telepathy exists. Although these dreams take place on the same night, they do not necessarily occur during the same period during that night. The following workshop example, in which four people dreamed similar dreams at various times throughout the night, contains remarkable similarities, and some interesting variations:

> *"German Shepherd"*
> *Dreamer No. 1: I'm in a room with some other people. A black-and-brown German shepherd runs*

up excitedly and jumps on me, licking my face. I think to myself that the dog should be sent to obedience school.

Dreamer No. 2: I'm in a room with [Dreamer No. 1]. A black-and-brown German shepherd runs up and jumps on me. It wags its tail and licks my face. I turn to [Dreamer No. 1] and say, "There's nothing wrong with this dog. He just needs to go to obedience school to learn where to lick!"

Dreamer No. 3: . . . A gray German shepherd runs in and jumps on me . . .

Dreamer No. 4: . . . A gray lamb runs into the room and jumps up on me . . .

Mutual dreams can also happen spontaneously, particularly when people share the same space during sleep, or have a close personal bond, as with partners or family members. One dreamer recalls an incident in his teenage years when a friend who had shared his room for the weekend recounted a dream almost identical to his! This type of dream may occur more often than we think, which is reason enough to share your dream stories with others. You never know when someone will say, "You know, I dreamed about the same thing last night!"

THE SCIENTIFIC STUDY OF PSI DREAMS

Interest in dreams as paranormal occurrences dates back thousands of years, to a time when dreams were considered to be prophecies that foretold of future events. By the nineteenth century, a "scientific" interest in psi dreams led to numerous experiments with precognition, clairvoyance, and telepathy. It was Montague Ullman who began in the 1960s what dream researcher Robert Van de Castle, himself a test subject, calls "the most systematic study of paranormal dreams in a laboratory setting." Working at Brooklyn's Maimonides Hospital, Ullman worked with psychologist Stanley Krippner to develop what would become the gold standard for other paranormal dream studies. Their 1970 book *Dream Studies and Telepathy* recounts their experiments and the often astonishing results.

Using a randomly selected target picture, a "sender" would sit in a locked room where no contact with the dreaming subject was possible; in fact, later experiments placed the subject fourteen miles away. When monitors indicated the beginning of a REM period, the sender would be signalled to awaken and concentrate on the target picture; when REM ended, the two participants would return to sleep. The following morning, the dreamer was asked to rank the likelihood of an illustration's being the target picture.

The results seemed more than coincidental. Although images were not always precise, as Van de Castle points out—"a full moon represented by a crystal ball, or a pencil by a telephone pole"—there was much similarity, especially given that there was absolutely zero contact between sender and recipient during the night of sleep.

Since these early experiments, researchers all over the world have continued to document and catalog psi dreams. In looking at psi dreams from a cultural perspective, Finnish folklore expert Leea Virtanen points out that cultural or folk beliefs can influence what a dream indicates to a particular dreamer. "If percipients have known from childhood that a certain dream about teeth indicates death [a popular Finnish folk belief], it is quite possible that feelings about death will take this form of expression in their dreams." Similarly, childhood beliefs may have had bearing on the "precognitive" dreams of a woman who reported to us that when she dreams of snow, she knows that personal crisis will occur that day in her waking life. "When I was a child,

my mother had some sort of card that had the different dream
interpretations on it, and snow was supposed to symbolize bad
tidings." In cases such as these, the symbol may appear when the
dreamer unconsciously perceives that some turmoil is about to
unfold. In these cases, whether the image appears as a pure indi-
cator of some future event is fairly difficult to discern. (This can
be frustrating for dedicated dreamworkers. But then again, these
mysteries are what make psi dreams so intriguing.)

In some ways, psi dreams are open to interpretation in much
the same way as other dreams. The metaphors we associate with
other kinds of dreams appear also in precognitive dreams,
Virtanen explains. We might dream, for instance, that someone
close to us leaves on a long journey, only to discover later that he
has died. Still, in at least 25 percent of psi dreams, she reports,
the events or circumstances depicted are "completely realistic."
"Usually," she writes, "the information is not limited to a simple
'X is dead,' or 'Y is ill and needs help'. . . . The realistic dream is
instead a vivid experience in which the dreamer learns dramatic
and specific details." Most often, these are details of a violent
attack, serious accident, or sudden illness; rarely, Virtanen says,
do people have psi dreams "about someone's "peaceful, 'natural' death."

IDENTIFYING YOUR PSI DREAMS

Sometimes, what seems like a psi dream may indeed be nothing
more than coincidence. The following dream about a car accident at first seemed like a psi dream, but further consideration
led the dreamer to conclude otherwise.

> *"Volvo Spin"*
> *I dream I am riding in my friend's silver Volvo with*
> *her and her daughter. We are in an accident, and*
> *the car begins spinning around and around in one*
> *place. We are shaken, but okay.*

"I had this dream on a Sunday night," reports the dreamer. "The next night, the tires on my gray Honda were slashed. I wondered whether there was any connection." It is sometimes confusing to try to figure out which dreams are psi dreams and which dreams are merely coincidental dreams. As always, the place to start is with the basic dream interpretation techniques discussed in this chapter. An examination of recent associations with the dream images (perhaps a feeling of "going around in circles"), previous experiences (being in a Volvo that wrecked), or upcoming plans (such as, a car trip with the friend) may net a meaningful interpretation that does not involve a psychic element at all. There are several plausible explanations for dreams that initially seem like psi dreams.

Previous but "forgotten" knowledge: Like Kekulé von Stradonitz, who had a dream that incorporated forgotten information that led to the discovery of benzene's molecular structure, you can know something (or theorize it), only to forget about it until it later surfaces in a dream. For example, a woman whose great-grandfather worked on a railroad repeatedly dreamed of an old man who reaches out a train window—a dream that was "cut off" at that point each time it recurred. Upon learning that the great-grandfather had died when he reached out to pick up a mailbag, the woman wondered whether she had experienced a psi dream. It is impossible to know, but worth speculating that she may have heard the details of the man's death while still a small child, only to forget them except in dreams.

Future plans: If you are planning to attend a conference, you may dream about participating on panels or in workshops, dining in the hotel restaurant, or other activities. Your fellow participants may do so as well. Does that mean you have experienced a mutual dream? Not necessarily. If the event you dream about is likely to occur in the future, the dream cannot be considered a true psi dream.

Sheer coincidence: Unless the dream depicts virtually the same event that later transpires, or is mirrored very closely by the other "mutual" dreamer, you can chalk it up to coincidence. The "Volvo Spin" dreamer, for instance, is unlikely to have experienced a psi dream: The events were not related closely enough.

So that's how you can begin to tell when it's *not* a psi dream. How do you know when it *is* one? Some frequent psi dreamers report a special quality to their psi dreams—an "old-time-movie" feel or an extremely vivid intensity (as with lucid dreams). Perhaps the best way to track your potential psi dreams is to keep a detailed dream journal, in which you have room to go back and connect dream images and events with happenings from your waking life.

"OUT-OF-BODY" EXPERIENCES

Some people experience dreams that are so vivid as to seem real: During these out-of-body experiences, or OBEs, they may see themselves as though an observer, perhaps rising up "out of" their bodies and hovering over themselves, or "traveling" bodilessly through the night to visit the bedroom of a sleeping friend. One man recalls an OBE that he still believes may have been "more than a dream":

> *"Floating and Flying"*
> *I rise up above my bed and look down at my body, which is still asleep. Then, I take off at great speed, flying through my bedroom into the adjacent master bathroom, toward the fireplace. I land on the floor, and look up to see my father, who appears to be the age he was when I was about five years old.*

He is shaving, and I watch him for a few minutes before flying back to my bed and slipping back into my sleeping body.

"Many people who have an OBE may have two conscious selves, one that remains in the body and participates in whatever activity is going on and one that floats above the body, a silent observer," explain Jayne Gackenbach and Jane Bosveld in *Control Your Dreams*. "When this sense of two selves occurs during sleep, some people may not realize they are sleeping, believing instead that they are awake, which of course they are— awake within a dream." The authors report that similar experiences occur when people meditate, take psychedelic drugs, and endure extreme stress.

NOCTURNAL HALLUCINATIONS

Have you ever had the experience of awakening from deep sleep and seeing something you can't explain? These nocturnal hallucinations may be dreams, but they are so exceptionally vivid that they can make those who have them wonder about the existence of ghosts. Leea Virtanen is one of the researchers who has studied hallucinations. "Seventy-five percent [of the visions we recorded] occurred in the borderline state between sleep and waking. Many of these visions seem to be continuations of dreams. The experience is usually very brief, perhaps only a few seconds. Typically, the apparition is perceived as a human form, which appears in the percipient's normal surroundings, [such as] in the bedroom." For instance, a young woman we interviewed recalls a time when she had just completed law school and was packing up her apartment for a move to Washington, D.C. On her final night in that apartment, she had an experience that still haunts her. She reports waking up in the middle of the night and looking toward her bedroom window, which was illuminated by a streetlight. As she began to focus her eyes, she saw a large human form step in front of the light, its back to her. At first, she told us, she thought it was an optical illusion, like a pile of clothes on a chair or a windblown drapery. But the room was empty, except for the bed and a dresser. She expected the "illusion" to fade away as her eyes adjusted to the dim light. Terrified, she froze in bed, then noticed the figure's long cloak and the heavy hood. "It looked like Death," she recalls. "As I started to look at the dresser mirror, to see whether I could see a face, the figure turned, and it was impossible to see. I turned on the light, and the figure was still there. Eventually, it did fade away, but I couldn't—wouldn't—go back to sleep." Was this a visit from a ghostly spectre? Or a symbolic dream or nightmare about the "death" of grad school life and the transition into the working world? Like other kinds of nightmares, experiences like this one are worth interpreting. But science has yet to verify or explain this phenomenon.

For some people, no explanation is sufficient; they truly believe they were in the presence of an otherworldly entity. For instance, another well-educated woman we know sublet her sister's New York City apartment only to have an experience so terrifying that she now sleeps with a crucifix over her bed to ward off evil. She reports waking up one night to feel an "evil presence" enter her room, climb onto the bed with her, and then proceed to sit on her chest in an apparent attempt to crush her. "I know it was evil," she says. "It's very hard for me to believe it was just a dream." Though she was quite shaken, she told a few friends about the incident at the time, and then ceased mentioning it. Imagine her surprise, though, when a few years later, she overheard her sister telling someone about a similar experience when she slept in that same bedroom!

Are such nighttime experiences merely dreams? Or are they waking encounters with otherworldly beings? To paraphrase famed University of Virginia psychiatrist Ian Stevenson, one of the world's foremost experts on parapsychology: It's not for us to determine whether there are ghosts; all we do is report what we hear. It is easy to define a dream as an experience we have while sleeping, but that simplistic definition becomes complicated when we are talking about experiences we have when we believe ourselves to have just awakened.

PSI DREAM EXPERIMENTS

It is possible to incubate psi dreams, much as you incubate creative dreams. Working with a friend or family member, you can attempt to collect your own anecdotal evidence of psi dreams without laboratory supervision. These experiments are simple, and fun to try, and may give you or your dream partner some valuable information about your waking life. Some experiments, like the one to follow, involve several friends or family members.

EXPERIMENT WITH TELEPATHY—IN PICTURES

This experiment, adapted from Phyllis Koch-Sheras's *Dream On,* is especially effective when you have the opportunity to dream together in close proximity—with overnight guests, for example, or on a camping trip.

You will need: Six pictures about the size of a standard 8½-by-11-inch piece of paper. These pictures should depict simple, identifiable subjects and be quite distinct from each other (such as a dog, a house, or a boat). You may cut the pictures out of a magazine or newspaper, or draw them clearly (or ask a talented participant to do so); remember, simplicity is key. You will also need pens and paper for the following morning, when the dreamers will record their dreams.

The procedure: One person agrees to be the sender and selects a target picture to transmit to the receivers as they sleep. The sender should concentrate on the image, visualizing it several times during the night. The sender could also envision a network connecting him or her with the receivers and sending the target picture in all directions. The receivers try to tune in to the picture as they are falling asleep, and give themselves a strong suggestion such as "Tonight, I will dream about the picture that is being sent my way."

The next morning, each receiver records his or her dreams privately, without saying anything to the sender or the other dreamers. The sender then shows all six pictures to the group, without comment; the sender might also offer some free associations he or she has with each illustration—these sometimes surface as part of the "message." Each dreamer then makes a guess as to which illustration was in fact the target picture, based on his or her own dream. Then, before the actual target picture is identified, each dreamer recounts his or her dream and tells which picture seems most closely associated with it.

Finally, the sender reveals which illustration is the target picture. All things being equal, the chance of guessing which is the target picture is one in six. It is interesting to discover how psi dreaming improves these odds.

EXPERIMENT WITH TELEPATHY—IN WORDS

For this experiment, you will need a receiver and a sender who is fully awake during the time the message is being sent. Again, a situation in which you are in the same location overnight is best. If you have a friend who is a night owl and you are a morning person, or if you sleep late and your friend arises early, you can coordinate your schedules so that this experiment works.

You will need: A piece of paper on which your friend can write down the message he or she intends to send you.

The procedure: Agree on a bedtime for the designated dreamer, and establish a game plan—for example, the sender may choose to sit outside the bedroom door, to sleep in the same room with the recipient, or whatever other arrangement might work.

Before the recipient goes to bed, the sender privately jots down a clear and specific message that he or she intends to send the recipient. The recipient then goes to sleep. At the agreed-upon time (for example, ninety minutes after the recipient is likely to have fallen asleep), the sender then concentrates on the message, repeating the words in his or her head. You can do this several times per night—if the sender is willing.

The next morning, the recipient writes down all dreams and fragments, attempting to exact a message. Afterward, the sender reveals the intended message.

EXPERIMENT WITH CLAIRVOYANCE

This experiment must be conducted solo, to avoid the interference of other dreamers and their dreams.

You will need: Twenty or thirty color pictures, cut out from magazines, simple in theme and content and dissimilar from one another. Insert each picture into a separate large manila envelope and shuffle them well.

The procedure: When you have thoroughly mixed the stack, select one envelope and mark the *back* of it with an X. Without looking at the contents, place the envelope under your pillow or mattress. Before going to sleep, give yourself the following suggestion: "I will dream about the picture I have selected, and when I wake up in the morning, I will remember the dream."

The next morning, record your dreams, then remove the envelope and shuffle it with five other pictures from your larger stack. Lay these six envelopes out, face up, so the backs don't show. Open each envelope and examine the pictures, placing each on its corresponding envelope. Decide which one is your target picture—the one you slept on overnight—then check the back of the envelope. You may well see a match!

These experiments are certainly fun to try. And, amazingly, they really can work. If you have established a dream group, you might suggest an overnight dream retreat in which group members can try some of these remarkable exercises. Families who are together for the holidays might also give these exercises a try. College roommates or other housemates might also make use of these techniques as a way of getting to know each other or just having fun. In the next chapter, we discuss other ways to share dream experiences, from establishing dream groups to co-dreaming with a partner or spouse. Dreams have power, psychic or otherwise, and sharing them with others only adds to that power.

CHAPTER NINE

DREAMWORK TEAMWORK
SHARING
YOUR DREAMS

By now, you understand how you can—and must—serve as the expert with the final say on your own dreams. Solitary dreamwork is a wonderful way to spend time alone, a tool for creative expression, a vehicle for self-exploration, and, for many, a time of meditation and focus. Sharing your dreams with others also has much to offer the dedicated dreamer. As you may have experienced, just recounting your dream to another person can cement it in your memory and make it come alive. And, as you might imagine, the reactions and associations someone else might have to your dream can lead you to new insights and observations. Finally, it can promote intimacy and closeness. Social dreamwork—dreamworking one on one or in a group—is not about having someone else interpret your dream for you. As you know, you are the source, and therefore the expert, on your own dreams. But imagine recounting a dream to an interested and supportive listener, then hearing that listener observe, "You seem like you really dislike that character. When you talk about her, your whole face tightens and you frown." You can then use this feedback to consider how your physical response relates to the dream's meaning.

Aside from offering support and potential new insights, social dreamwork offers the chance to practice your dream interpretation skills. Encouragement from others helps to keep these skills alive. Like sharing a personal story with a friend or loved one, sharing dreams with each other can enhance your relationship and build closeness and understanding, adding value to the dream itself. Montague Ullman, an important innovator of group dreamwork techniques, puts it this way: "The paradox of dreamwork is that the dream, the product of our most private and intimate being, can best be brought to fullest realization through being shared with another or others. The helpful outside emotional support and the stimulation of imaginative input brings the dreamer closer to his own production."

> *EVEN SLEEPERS ARE WORKERS AND COLLABORATORS IN WHAT GOES ON IN THE UNIVERSE."*
> *—Heraclitus, seventh-century B.C. Greek philosopher*

This kind of supportive listening can help to create the kind of safety and structure required for the deep inner work necessary for accessing the unconscious. Carl Jung called this safe, protective space *temenos,* which is a Greek word meaning "the precincts of a sacred temple"; Jungian psychoanalysts still use the term to refer to the special framework psychoanalysis provides. One such analyst, Karen Signell, suggests that you can think of dream temenos as the special "place" that is created when you share a dream with a committed listener. This forum for dreamwork can motivate you to explore your dream further than you would alone. A committed listener or group of listeners provides a level of empathy and concern that makes deep dream-work possible. If at any point you feel hesitant to continue working on something in a particular dream, state these feelings, then set the dream aside for a while; the material will always be there when you are ready to continue.

Another benefit of dream-sharing is that it helps you to integrate the dream message into your waking life. Senoi dream-work, you will remember, reportedly involved daily dream-sharing that helped dreamers incorporate their dream life into their waking existence. Negative feelings or images associated with another tribe member were shared and then transformed into something positive. The Senoi were a relatively harmonious people for many generations, and some researchers believe it was because they shared their dreams. In today's world, we too can connect with the members of our human family through social dreamwork. Sharing dream stories helps to bring the symbols of waking-life conflicts, fears, and wishes to the surface, where you can discuss them, receive emotional support, and take actions to address them.

Finally, sharing dreams regularly makes it possible to explore the phenomena of mutual dreams and psychic events, perhaps discovering themes both you and your dream "partner" explored in dreams the night before, perhaps looking for ways in which your dream might have predicted an event or led to a new revelation. Imagine your amazement when you discover that you and a friend had the "same" dream, or a very similar one, on a particular night!

The beauty of dream-sharing is that you need not have a firm grasp on the meaning of your dream before you share it. Nor must you understand another person's dream in order to be of help. Just swapping dream stories can lead to new areas of exploration and build friendship and community among fellow dream-sharers. There are several options for those interested in creating a format for sharing dreams. In fact, you may have already started—by sharing your dreams informally, regaling your household members at the breakfast or dinner table with tales from the dreamworld, checking in with a friendly co-worker during a mid-morning coffee break, or sharing a dream story with your child on the way to school. Social dreamwork can happen at any time, in any place, with any number of people. It's just a matter of your being willing to share, and someone else's being willing to listen.

DREAM-SHARING WITH A FRIEND

"I had the wildest dream last night . . . " So often, we turn to a friend or co-worker to recount the tale of a dream adventure. Dreams can be entertaining, puzzling, or disturbing, and it's natural to recount them much as we do our waking experiences. Whether shared informally in this way, or presented with a plan for gaining insight into their meaning, dreams are appealing food for thought and discussion. There are special advantages, however, to setting up a regularly scheduled "dreamtime" with a friend, a time in which each of you has the chance to recount dreams and explore their possible meanings in the company of a committed listener; that is, someone who agrees to support you fully and attentively, without interruption (sometimes called an "active listener").

Co-author Phyllis Koch-Sheras has been doing dreamwork with the same friend for more than seventeen years, meeting every other week for a one-on-one session that has netted some wonderful results. Although she does not have professional expertise in dreamwork, Koch-Sheras's dreamwork partner has similar goals and interest in working on dreams. They developed their own format for working together, which is outlined here:

Connection: The partners sit facing each other, and may hold hands as a way of feeling connected or grounded. They divide the time in half, and decide who will go first, generally alternating unless someone has a special need.

New and good: Taking turns, they begin each session by stating the new and good things that have occurred since the last time they met. This step helps each person to focus on their present experience, and to find something good even in the most miserable of weeks, which is good practice for turning disturbing dream images into productive messages.

The dream report: Next, the first speaker recounts a dream in the present tense, then in dream language, commenting on the feeling at the end, and giving the dream a title. (Note: It is best to retell the dream, rather than just reading the dream as written in the dream journal, because new details may come out in the retelling.) The person then chooses a dream character or object to role-play, acting it out and then asking it for a message. If the dreamer wishes, he or she might ask the listening partner to "be" a character to whom the dreamer is speaking in order to create immediacy. The speaker goes on to role-play other parts of the dream and to change or finish the dream if appropriate. The second partner begins his or her turn only after the first partner has completed all steps of the process, managing the amount of time available.

Undivided attention: Each partner listens intently to the other without interruption, unless the speaker seems to be ignoring something obvious or is at a loss as to where to go next. At that time, the listener can interject a direction or suggestion, but remains otherwise silent as the work continues. For example, if the dreamer omits a part of the dream when translating it into dream language, the listener should point out what has been left out and have the speaker go back and include it. (Often people "forget" a dream element that turns out to be an important clue to the meaning of the dream.) The only other interruption would be to signal the speaking partner that time is almost up or the turn is over. (If there isn't enough time to complete the dreamwork, the speaker can negotiate for more time or make an agreement to complete the dreamwork alone at a later time.)

Actions to take: Often, a dream will give rise to some change the dreamer wishes to make in waking life. So it is helpful to end each dreamwork session with a commitment to take a certain action before the next meeting. At the beginning of the next session, the results of this action are reported.

Looking forward to: Each dreamer takes a moment at the end of his or her turn to focus on positive upcoming events, a final step that helps make the transition from the realm of dreams back into the realm of waking life.

When establishing this kind of partnership, it's a good idea to agree on some basic ground rules, such as where and when to meet (you can alternate locations, but choose a quiet one where you can speak freely without distraction), how often and how long each session will be, what to do if a partner is late (two options: forego some of your time if you're tardy, or divide the remaining time in half). As you work with your partner, you can adapt this format to your own needs and experiences.

Koch-Sheras's dream partner says she finds several benefits from working with a partner. "One of the great things about working together is I *do* it. I wouldn't work on my dreams anywhere near as frequently if we weren't meeting. The fact that we're both taking the time to sit down, tell our dreams, put them into dream language, and offer each other suggestions is very useful." She also values the self-directed format they have devised. "It's a very unintrusive way of working together," she says. "We can work side by side—we don't interrupt very often, but when we do it makes the experience more powerful. We are really trying to help the other person, rather than express our own agenda or interpretation."

Social dreamwork has special significance when you are sharing a dream with someone (such as a friend, family member, or co-worker) who appeared as a character in it. Because dreams tend to reflect your feelings about the people in your life, their appearance in your dreams is likely to reveal your true perceptions of them. Discussing them as dream characters will help you to understand how you see them, both favorably and unfavorably. And of course, the part of you that the dream character represents is worthy of discussion, too—considering that what you see in them is really a "projection" of part of yourself onto another.

This kind of work can lead to a new level of understanding and sympathy (seeing things from another's perspective). Social dreamwork is a gentle way to explore such issues in a friendly forum. Resolving whatever conflict occurs in a dream between yourself and another dream character helps to clear up conflicts between the two of you in waking life, especially those you had not yet "put a finger on" or acknowledged. (The Senoi were said to apologize to each other for arguments that occurred in their dreams!)

DREAM-SHARING AS A COUPLE

In many ways, it's easiest to share dreams with the person you wake up next to, and many couples make it a practice to share their dreams each morning. Tuning in to your dreams can enable you and your partner to understand each other better, enhancing intimacy by providing an opportunity, whether occasional or regular, for identifying and talking about your concerns. Recounting your dream adventures is a wonderful way to con-

nect with each other before going your separate ways for the
day. In these days of busy schedules and hectic workweeks,
dream-sharing is a good way to touch base. It can also help couples deal with some of the more difficult areas of relating.

Often, couples get stuck negotiating to get their needs met.
Traditional roles and typical patterns in the relationship lead to
stalemate, which can be extremely frustrating for both partners.
Even when you don't know the answer, your dreams might offer
clues and solutions that will really work in your waking life. For
instance, a woman engaged to be married was at a loss as to how
to share the space and responsibilities of the home she and her
fiancé were moving in to. Then she had this dream.

"Eight Tennis Balls"

*My fiancé is going to be in a contest that involves
doing something with eight tennis balls. There are
only four balls in the can. I tell him that he doesn't
have to worry about the other four balls because I
already did those. That will make it easier for us
to win.*

"The house we bought had eight rooms in it," she explains.
"And we were in the midst of figuring out how to divide them
up and share the responsibilities for the upkeep of the house
fairly. This dream helped me realize we could divide things up
equally (both the physical space and the responsibilities) and
that I could feel good about that—even though it was very different from what I had been taught and had done in the past." In
sharing this dream with her husband-to-be, this dreamer realized
there was a new way to do things, one that served to enhance
their relationship. Over the years, they have had to modify how
they share responsibilities in their relationship, but the dream
still serves to remind them that there are always new ways to
work together to keep all the "balls" in the air!

Conflicts of all kinds are an inevitable part of being a couple, and dreams can play a central role in their resolution. The first step in resolving a conflict is to take responsibility for your part of it. Dreamwork offers a perfect opportunity to put a conflict to rest by first "owning" the dream and all aspects of it—including the character of your partner—as part of yourself. If you dream about your partner as being cold, distant, and mechanical, stop to consider the cold, distant, and mechanical parts of yourself, and what role they might be playing (or need to play) in your waking life. Using dream language and sharing the results with your partner, you can begin to express and acknowledge your own part in having things be the way they are.

One man who was having trouble telling his wife how upset he was about several things in their relationship dreamed he divorced her. He mustered up the courage to tell his wife about the dream, using it to open up a discussion of their problems. He explained he was "divorcing himself" from communicating some important thoughts and feelings, and told her how afraid he was that they were drifting apart. With the dream to get them started, this couple found a way to work on the issues in their waking life.

From a sexual standpoint, dreams can be quite revealing, but not always in the ways that you might think. Sharing dreams of sexuality can enhance the physical connection with your partner in a number of ways. For one thing, just sharing the sexual or erotic dream itself can enable you to overcome inhibitions and increase your sexual enjoyment. Dreams can also bring to light sexual needs you might be afraid to express or admit. And remember, nothing is just as it seems in dreams, so an erotic or sexual dream about someone other than a partner, even a parent or member of the same sex, is often merely an expression of your acceptance or interest in communing with the parent or same-sex part of yourself, and not necessarily an expression of hidden desires for the actual person. Keep this in mind as your partner recounts his or her dreams, and never express disapproval of your partner's sexual choices in dreams. Instead, become curious about them, and think of them as gifts of insight and intimacy.

Couples need not wait for a dream to "happen" to them—they can seek out a solution by incubating a dream using some of the techniques in chapter 6. Jointly programming both of your dreaming minds to address a particular issue is a practice we call co-dreaming. A couple with young children used this process during a vacation, when they wanted to create more available time for each other and their children. They agreed to incubate their dreams to discover a solution, and to work together to interpret the dreams after they had occurred. In a dream one of them had, each child appeared with a twin, suggesting to the couple that the children could be twice as helpful as they had been, giving the family four people to help out instead of two. Delegating routine chores among the four family members meant more free time. They put their idea into action immediately, and packing up to go home was much more efficient, giving everyone more time to enjoy the last hours of their trip together.

Couples dreamwork is not all about problem-solving and conflict resolution. Dreams also contain messages of closeness and connection, and it is just as important to highlight those. Dreams may lead you to see special areas in your relationship that you may not have noticed or acknowledged in the past. When you have a nice dream about your partner—in which he or she is loving, protective, triumphant, sexy, whatever—let your partner know. When your partner shares such a dream with you, take it as a gift, and bring it into your waking life in some concrete ways. You may find some wonderful opportunities for living out the fantasies of your dreams!

DREAMWORK WITH CHILDREN

Much has been written about ways to forge the bond between parent and child. Throughout your child's life, from babyhood on, dependence and rebellion ebb and flow like the tide. Through it all, you want to stay close to your child, to understand his or her needs, emotionally and physically, and to do what you can to meet them. Your child's dreams are a world of symbolic images that offer clues you can discuss and analyze together whenever you wish. Valuing your child's dreams encourages self-expression and provides an easy point of departure for a discussion of any number of issues. As soon as your children are old enough to tell you what they have dreamed, you can begin to discuss dreams with them.

Particularly where nightmares are concerned, looking for hints of conflict and confusion is part of being a concerned parent. Take your child's nightmare experience seriously, and listen carefully as he or she expresses fear. Nightmares are extraordinarily vivid, and the emotions in them are real, particularly to a child too young to distinguish between fantasy and reality. Indeed, some 40 percent of the dreams children remember are nightmares, and they may be dealing with some important developmental issues through them, so it's simply not enough to say to them, "Go back to sleep, it was only a dream."

Indeed, there is much to gain from listening to your children's dreams. One little boy, for instance, at age three had a dream that allowed the family to address issues surrounding the pending birth of a second child. He dreamed his mother was a "scary clown" with a painted face and one big nipple on her neck. In the dream, both son and father tell the clown to go away. Talking about the dream together led the mother to ask the boy whether he thought she would have enough "milk"—time, energy, and love—for the whole family after the new baby was born. Imagine their surprise when their son said, "No, I think there won't be enough for the baby!" This comment clued both parents in to the child's feelings of jealousy, and his desire to keep the baby "in its place." As a family, they were able to work through these issues in anticipation of conflict.

A child's night terror is something else entirely. During these episodes, a child may not remember any dream details, instead reporting or displaying a general feeling of extreme fear. He or she may scream, make choking sounds, sweat, or feel paralyzed, sensations that can be terrifying in and of themselves. "This disorder upsets parents more than the victim, who usually does not remember the event," writes Patricia Garfield in *Your Child's Dreams,* "[however] any actions parents can take to increase the child's sense of security and well-being [in waking life] are worthwhile." If the child exhibits these symptoms without waking up, let him or her sleep through it if possible. Experts advise against asking the awakened child to explore any associations to it, urging parents to comfort and calm the child until he or she returns to sleep. You might give some thought yourself to any areas of conflict or anxiety in the child's life, but rather than discuss your concerns with your child, simply assure the child that everything is all right, and it's safe to go back to bed. Night terrors generally disappear by the teenage years. Experts believe treatment is ineffective and may only serve to make the child anxious. Patience, they say, is the best cure.

Perhaps the best way to encourage your children to talk freely about their dreams is to share some of yours on a regular basis. Tell them a dream, talk about the feelings the dream gave you, and what new things you learned from the dream. Hearing you express your genuine emotions—excitement, joy, fear, sadness—sends the message that it's okay to feel these things, in dreams and in waking life. Of course, you'll want to consider

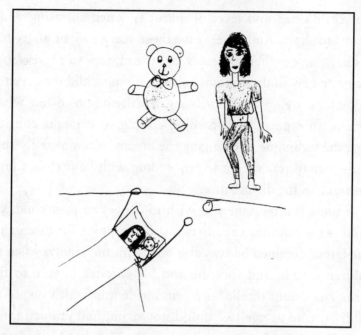

Figures 9.1, 9.2: *These dream drawings were made during a children's dreamwork session with co-author Phyllis Koch-Sheras, who suggested that the children invent a dream helper character who could assist and protect them in their dreams.*

your child's age and level of maturity when choosing which dreams to share. And never leave those scary, sad, or angry feelings hanging out there unresolved; instead, seek to express some clarity or new understanding, showing your child that even an unpleasant dream has something worthwhile to offer. Where there is an especially disturbing ending, you might consider using the technique of changing the dream to complete the message—perhaps creating a happy ending with your child's input that resolves the disturbance.

If there is a message you wish to convey to your child, you could use a relevant dream as a starting point for discussion. One father dreamed he was at a lake with the family; when the children dive in and sink, he and his wife try in vain to find them. The dream recalled a recent incident in which one of the children, who at age two could not swim, had jumped into a pool. The father had jumped in to save him, but his feeling of panic remained, surfacing again in the dream. Recounting the dream to his children was an excellent way to express his fear, and convey the seriousness of water safety to them. Together, they added an ending in which the father rescues both children. They also agreed to arrange for swimming lessons as soon as possible.

Psychological interpretation may seem like a tall order for most children. But when discussed in simple terms, emotions are an appropriate topic even with young children; talking about dream emotions is good practice for identifying and managing emotions in waking life. Making dreamwork into imaginative play is a good way to encourage this special kind of storytelling, and that's where some of the more playful approaches to dream interpretation come in handy. Your child can dialogue with dream characters or act out the dream, then talk about how it feels to do so.

Many of the dreamwork exercises we have discussed are appropriate for children. Children of any age can keep a dream journal; if they are too young to write, you can transcribe their dream stories, leaving room if you wish for accompanying dream drawings. Dream drawings or collages can also stand alone, of course. Sometimes, your children may wish to write stories or make drawings based on dreams, changing their endings or creating new adventures with the same characters or settings. They may also enjoy creating a dream helper whose assistance they can enlist before going to sleep or while in the dream; a teddy bear makes a good dream helper, but so does an imagined character; ask them who they would like their dream helper to be. Page 221 shows some illustrations children have done in response to this idea—as part of a children's dream workshop Phyllis Koch-Sheras conducts in which children invent a character called "Dreamme" as their personal dream helper and protector.

Dreamwork is fun. Children don't need to know it is also "good for them." It's enough for *you* to know that it is good for them, and for you, too. Your children's dream play can clue you in to the issues they face as they grow and change. What's more, dreamwork is an enjoyable family activity that can become a lifelong tradition. Over time, your children will begin to appreciate and nurture their own inner lives, looking to their dreamworlds for answers when their waking worlds offer none, and enjoying their dream adventures rather than discounting them or, worse, fearing their outcomes. Together, family dreamworkers can nurture, support, and learn from one another.

WORKING WITH A DREAM GROUP

Unlike the Senoi, we don't usually have the chance to participate in regular, structured dreamwork sessions as part of our daily

lives. But where there's a will, there's a way, and we encourage
you to think about ways to explore dreams with friends, neigh-
bors, co-workers, church or synagogue members, or other
groups. Whether it's a one-time dream storytelling session or a
regular meeting with a set format, working with some kind of
dream group has much to offer. As they say, two heads are better
than one; more heads can be even better. Your fellow dreamworkers can listen to your dream, observe your body posture as
you recount it, ask questions, allow you to dialogue with them
as the dream characters, play out your different dream roles, and
give you feedback on how they felt when they were acting out
these different people or objects.

As psychologist Montague Ullman points out in the introduction to his book on group dreamwork, *Working with
Dreams,* people who are not "personally involved" in a dream
can more freely associate to the symbols in the dream because,
he says, "they do not have to deal with the consequences of their
reading." Where you, the dreamer might downplay an association to a symbol for fear of having to confront it head on, a
group member might tread freely into this somewhat dangerous
territory, without the inhibition the dreamer would feel. Nor are
your fellow dreamworkers hampered by the same prejudices or
past experiences that you are.

If you are interested in becoming part of a dream group, you
might first check local resources to find out whether there is an
existing group with an opening (contact psychological associations, check for a flier at your local library, inquire at a nearby
university or community college, and ask around!). Or start
your own group. It's not as hard as it sounds. You could invite
friends or professionals who might be interested in dreams, dis-
tribute fliers around college campuses or the town center, or
send a press release listing an introductory meeting in a public
place, open to all who are interested.

At your first meeting, begin by discussing these questions:

1. What does each person want from the group?

2. Does anyone have experience with working in a dream group?

3. Will the group limit the number of members? How long will the meetings be? (We recommend four to eight regular members meeting one and a half to four hours per session.)

4. How often will you meet? (Regular sessions help to build a rapport and keep everyone interested.)

5. Where will you meet? (We recommend a comfortable location where you will not be disturbed, such as a university or library lounge, a church or other community recreation room, or, if you prefer, someone's home.)

6. Will the group be of the same sex, or mixed? (Sharing in a same-sex group tends to be easier and more free-flowing for many people.)

7. What ground rules will there be? (Keeping a dream journal, arriving on time, taking turns on different nights, not smoking or eating during sessions, keeping the dreamwork confidential, etc. Discuss these options to determine preferences.)

8. How will you monitor time? (Especially with larger groups, time is hard to keep track of. You want to agree on enough time for each dream and for the entire session, including all necessary follow-up, so you might want to identify whether a particular dream is highly emotional and perhaps best addressed at the beginning of a session rather than at the end.)

At first, you may hesitate to bare your soul to other group members. Trust takes time, and establishing ground rules helps to build that trust. A set format also helps you build confidence and increase your comfort level. We suggest using the following model as a basis for designing your session framework.

Sit in a circle: Eye contact is important, and so is enough room to get up and move around as necessary.

Start with what's new and good: Go around the circle, giving all group members a chance to talk about what is new and good, how they feel right then, what their dream lives have been like, and whether they have dreams to share that session. (Be sure to monitor your time for this.)

Share a dream: Have one person tell a dream in the present tense, and then in dream language. It's preferable not to read directly from the dream journal, though a dreamer might wish to refer back to it to check for accuracy or jog the memory. After telling the dream, the dreamer gives it a title and offers comments such as associations to the symbols, relation to the previous day or two, or similarities to previous dreams. If the dreamer has made a dream drawing or other creative piece based on the dream, he or she can introduce it here.

Amplify the dream: Other members can discuss the dream, ask questions using Ullman's "If it were my dream" technique, and commenting on the dreamer's body language as he or she recounted the dream. Now is the time to employ techniques such as those described in chapter 6—dialoguing, role-playing, and finishing or changing the dream.

End with follow-up: Bring each dreamworker's turn to a proper close before moving on to the next person. Ullman says this important phase of group dreamwork "involves returning the dream to the dreamer," who sums up what he or she has learned during the session, and asks any remaining questions.

(Group members, too, might wish to share what they have gained from another's dream.) The dreamer might make a resolution for future action based on the dreamwork, with the intention of reporting the results in a later session.

It may seem awkward at first to share your dreams so completely with other people. So building trust among group members is important. Scheduling some related events outside the workshop is a way to "team-build" and foster camaraderie. Some suggestions: Visit a gallery to study artwork based on dreams, hold an overnight dream retreat, or invite a guest speaker to lecture or lead a workshop. Over time, your friendships will deepen and grow, creating support for each person and strengthening the bond of the entire group. It is also all right to have no other social contact with your dream group members; you may wish to keep the group a special, separate part of your life. Explore with your group what feels most comfortable for you.

SHARING A GUIDED FANTASY

Another way to share your dreams and learn more about yourself is to use your own dreams to create a guided fantasy for others to follow. With your dream as the raw material, you can present all the elements in a way that helps your partner or group members experience the fantasy much like you experienced the dream. Hearing what they have to say about the fantasy can give you insight into the original dream, deepening your understanding of it, and can also give others an intimate, enriching experience to share with you. These tips can help get you started:

C Relax your listeners, perhaps playing some soothing instrumental music. Ask them to get

into a comfortable position, then encourage them
to take some deep breaths.

◐ Make the fantasy vivid. Include sights, sounds,
smells, tastes, movements, and other details that
involve your listeners' senses.

◐ Keep it flowing. Use smooth transitions from one
scene to the next. (If you think of it as a movie,
you will be able to picture smooth versus rough
breaks from scene to scene.)

◐ Edit carefully. If there are specific dream elements that might distract from the mood or
theme you are trying to convey, leave them out.

◐ End with a neutral or positive scene. Lead your
listeners up to the point of conflict, giving them
the chance to create their own ending, or change
the ending of your original dream in a positive
way. Notice their reactions and interpretations.

DREAMWORK WITH A THERAPIST

Dreams are a fertile ground for understanding our own psyches,
and they may reveal to us from time to time emotions and conflicts that professional counseling or therapy of some kind might
help resolve. If for any reason you want or feel you need professional guidance from a therapist, we encourage you to seek it.
After all, psychotherapeutic consultation is not reserved for
those who are disturbed or out of control. Personal growth is a
positive goal, so desiring help with a particular issue that surfaces in your dreams is reason enough to consult a professional.
A dreamworker who comes to a standstill after working on

dreams alone or with friends may wish to develop a new level of awareness or understanding by working with a therapist.

Therapy is a good place to take your questions and feelings about the parts of yourself that are difficult or unpleasant to confront as they make themselves known through your dreams. A competent therapist, one who is experienced in working with dreams, can help you integrate the darker and lighter sides of yourself, using dreams as food for thought and discussion. Consult your state psychological association for referral to a psychologist or other mental health professional who lists a particular interest in dreamwork, or shop around, based on a friend's or physician's recommendations. And remember, you have the right to ask a prospective therapist about interests, qualifications, and background.

IN CONCLUSION:
A COMMUNITY OF DREAMERS

In dreams, we take the walls down, opening ourselves up to the infinite possibilities within us. Some of these explorations are pleasant, some are horrifying, some are mundane, and some seem downright silly. All of them are our own creations; all of them have ourselves as the source. With *The Dream Sourcebook's* tools at hand, you have the expertise to learn the language and customs of your own personal dreamworld, and the passport you need to visit that world in the mode of explorer and diplomat, negotiating for the ultimate truth that empowers your dreaming and waking lives.

Throughout this book, there are opportunities for you to enlist your dreams to work with you to achieve a more integrated waking and dreaming life. You now know more about what happens when you dream, what the world's cultures have believed about dreams, and what contemporary researchers and theorists have concluded. You know that you can use dreams to explore the frontiers of human consciousness, to solve problems, to foster creative expression, and to promote understanding and intimacy with family and friends. As the great psychiatrist Carl Jung wrote in *Man and His Symbols,* "The interpretation of dreams and symbols demands intelligence. It cannot be turned into a mechanical system and then crammed into unimaginative brains." *The Dream Sourcebook* provides you with the information and techniques you need to awaken your mind's imagination to working with your own dreams, collecting the gifts from your dreamworld and presenting them to your waking self.

> *"THE FUTURE BELONGS TO THOSE WHO BELIEVE IN THE BEAUTY OF THEIR DREAMS."*
> *—Eleanor Roosevelt, former first lady*

Dreams can inspire growth and change, in yourself, and in others. Choices become conscious. Feelings become clear. Actions become obvious. Integrating the messages you receive from your dreams into your waking life can enrich your *entire* life. The dreamworld is a world all your own. Go there, find the source, and bring it back to your waking life to share with all.

APPENDIX A
BIBLIOGRAPHY

INTRODUCTION

Faraday, Ann. *Dream Power.* New York: Coward, McCann & Geoghegan, Inc., 1972.

Koch-Sheras, Phyllis R., E. Ann Hollier et al. *Dream On: A Dream Interpretation and Exploration Guide for Women.* Englewood Cliffs, NJ: Prentice-Hall, 1983.

Perls, Frederick "Fritz." *Gestalt Therapy Verbatim.* New York: Bantam Books, 1971.

CHAPTER 1

Bell, Alison. *The Dream Scene.* Los Angeles: Lowell House, 1994.

Cartwright, Rosalind D. *Night Life: Explorations in Dreaming.* Englewood Cliffs, NJ: Prentice-Hall, 1977.

Dement, William C. *Some Must Watch while Some Must Sleep.* New York: W.W. Norton & Company, 1972.

Dolnick, Edward. "What Dreams Are (Really) Made Of." *The Atlantic Monthly* (July 1990).

Faraday, Ann. *Dream Power.* New York: Coward, McCann & Geoghegan, Inc., 1972.

Freud, Sigmund. *The Interpretation of Dreams*. New York: Basic Books, 1953.

Gackenbach, Jayne, and Jane Bosveld. *Control Your Dreams*. New York: Harper & Row, 1989.

Hobson, J. Allan. *The Dreaming Brain*. New York: Basic Books, 1988.

Kastner, Jonathan, and Marianna Kastner. *Sleep: The Mysterious Third of Your Life*. New York: Harcourt, Brace & World Inc., 1968.

Kinoshite, June. "Dreams of a Rat: The Role of Dreams in Human Survival." *Discover* (July 1992).

Koch-Sheras, Phyllis R. et al. *Dream On: A Dream Interpretation and Exploration Guide for Women*. Englewood Cliffs, NJ: Prentice-Hall, 1983.

Ullman, Montague, and Nan Zimmerman. *Working with Dreams*. London: Hutchinson and Co., 1979.

Van de Castle, Robert. *Our Dreaming Mind*. New York: Ballantine Books, 1994.

Woods, Ralph L., and Herbert B. Greenhouse, eds. *The New World of Dreams*. New York: Macmillan Publishing Company, 1974.

———. "Common Questions About Nightmares." Vienna, VA: Association for the Study of Dreams, 1990.

———. "Common Questions About Dreams." Vienna, VA: Association for the Study of Dreams, 1990.

———. "National Institute of Mental Health Research on Sleep and Dreams." Washington, D.C.: U.S. Department of Health, Education, and Welfare, 1976.

CHAPTER 2

Bell, Alison. *The Dream Scene*. Los Angeles: Lowell House, 1994.

Boxer, Sarah. "Inside Our Sleeping Minds." *Modern Maturity* (October–November 1989).

Dolnick, Edward. "What Dreams Are (Really) Made Of." *The Atlantic Monthly* (July 1990).

Domhoff, G. William. *The Mystique of Dreams: A Search for Utopia through Senoi Dream Theory,* Berkeley, CA: University of California Press, 1985.

Daldianus, Artemidorus. *The Interpretation of Dreams: Oneirocritica*. Translated by Robert J. White. Torrance, CA: Original Books, 1990.

Das Gupta, Krishna. *The Shadow World: A Study of Ancient and Modern Dream Theories*. Delhi: Atma Ram & Sons, 1971.

de Becker, Raymond. *The Understanding of Dreams*. New York: Hawthorn Books, Inc., 1968.

Garfield, Patricia. *Creative Dreaming*. New York: Ballantine Books, 1974.

Gouda, Yehia. *Dreams and Their Meanings in the Arab Tradition*. New York: Vantage Press, 1991.

Hastings, James, ed., *Dictionary of the Bible*. New York: Charles Scribners, 1963.

Hirsch, E. D., Jr. et al. *The Dictionary of Cultural Literacy: What Every American Needs to Know*. Boston: Houghton Mifflin Company, 1993.

Jedrej, M. C., and Rosalind Shaw, eds. *Dreaming, Religion, and Society in Africa*. Leiden, the Netherlands: E.J. Brill, 1992.

Kastner, Jonathan, and Marianna Kastner. *Sleep: The Mysterious Third of Your Life*. New York: Harcourt, Brace & World Inc., 1968.

Kelsey, Morton T. *God, Dreams, and Revelation: A Christian Interpretation of Dreams*. Minneapolis: Augsburg Publishing House, 1995.

Koch-Sheras, Phyllis R. et al. *Dream On: A Dream Interpretation and Exploration Guide for Women*. Englewood Cliffs, NJ: Prentice-Hall, 1983.

Miller, Gustavus Hindman. *A Dictionary of Dreams: An Alphabetical Journey Through the Images of Sleep*. New York: Smithmark Publishers Inc., 1994.

Van de Castle, Robert L. *Our Dreaming Mind*. New York: Ballantine Books, 1994.

Von Grunebaum, G. E., and Roger Caillois, eds. *The Dream and Human Societies*. Berkeley, CA: University of California Press, 1966.

Woods, Ralph L., and Herbert B. Greenhouse. *The New World of Dreams*. New York: Macmillan, 1974.

CHAPTER 3

Appignanesi, Richard. *Freud for Beginners*. New York: Pantheon, 1979.

Boss, Medard. *The Analysis of Dreams*. New York: Philosophical Library, 1958.

de Becker, Raymond. *The Understanding of Dreams*. New York: Hawthorn Books, Inc., 1968.

Dolnick, Edward. "What Dreams Are (Really) Made Of." *The Atlantic Monthly* (July 1990).

Freud, Sigmund. *The Interpretation of Dreams*. New York: Basic Books, 1953.

Gackenbach, Jayne, and Jane Bosveld. *Control Your Dreams*. New York: Harper & Row, 1989.

Gendlin, Eugene. *Let Your Body Interpret Your Dreams*. Wilmette, IL: Chiron Publications, 1986.

Gutheil, Emil A. *The Handbook of Dream Analysis*. New York: Liveright, 1951.

Hall, Calvin. *The Meaning of Dreams*. New York: McGraw-Hill Book Company, 1966.

Hobson, J. Allan. *The Dreaming Brain*. New York: Basic Books, 1988.

Kinoshite, June. "Dreams of a Rat: The Role of Dreams in Human Survival." *Discover* (July 1992).

Jones, Richard M. *The New Psychology of Dreaming*. New York: Grune & Stratton, 1970.

Jung, Carl G. "The Archetypes and the Collective Unconscious." In *The Collected Works of C. G. Jung*, vol. 9, Part I, translated by R.F.C. Hull, Bollinger Series XX, Princeton, NJ: Princeton University Press, 1969.

Keleman, Stanley. "The Dream," unpublished work, Berkeley, CA, 1993.

Krippner, Stanley, and Joseph Dillard. *Dreamworking: How to Use Your Dreams for Creative Problem-Solving*. New York: Bearly Limited, 1988.

Mindell, Arnold. *Working on Yourself Alone: Inner Dreambody Work*. New York: Penguin Books, 1990.

Norbu, Namkhai. *Dream Yoga and the Practice of Natural Light.* Ithaca, NY: Snow Lion Publications, 1992.

Perls, Frederick. S. *Gestalt Therapy Verbatim.* New York: Bantam Books, 1971.

Stekel, Wilhelm. *The Interpretation of Dreams.* New York: Grosset & Dunlap, 1962.

Ullman, Montague, and Nan Zimmerman. *Working with Dreams.* London: Hutchinson and Co., 1979.

Van de Castle. *Our Dreaming Mind.* New York: Ballantine Books, 1994.

CHAPTER 4

Bell, Alison. *The Dream Scene.* Los Angeles: Lowell House, 1994.

Bethards, Betty. *The Dream Book: Symbols for Self-Understanding.* Novato, CA: Inner Light Foundation, 1983.

Koch-Sheras, Phyllis R. et al. *Dream On: A Dream Interpretation and Exploration Guide for Women.* Englewood Cliffs, NJ: Prentice-Hall, 1983.

Norbu, Namkhai. *Dream Yoga and the Practice of Natural Light.* Ithaca, NY: Snow Lion Publications, 1992.

Rubinstein, Kenneth, and Stanley Krippner. "Gender Differences and Geographical Differences in Content from Dreams Elicited by a Television Announcement." *Journal of Psychosomatics,* vol. 38 (1991).

CHAPTER 5

de Becker, Raymond. *The Understanding of Dreams.* New York: Hawthorn Books, 1968.

Faraday, Ann. *Dream Power.* New York: Coward, McCann & Geoghegan, Inc., 1972.

Ibid., *The Dream Game.* New York: Harper & Row Publishers, 1974.

Gendlin, Eugene. *Let Your Body Interpret Your Dreams.* Wilmette, IL: Chiron Publications, 1986.

Jung, Carl G. *Man and His Symbols.* New York: Dell, 1964.

Koch-Sheras, Phyllis R. et al. *Dream On: A Dream Interpretation and Exploration Guide for Women*. Englewood Cliffs, NJ: Prentice-Hall, 1983.

Signell, Karen A. *Wisdom of the Heart: Working with Women's Dreams*. New York: Bantam, 1990.

Weir, John. "The Personal Growth Laboratory." Kenneth Benne et al., eds. *The Laboratory Method of Changing and Learning: Theory and Application*. Palo Alto, CA: Science and Behavior Books, Inc., 1975.

CHAPTER 6

Bulkeley, Kelly. "The Reality of Castaneda's Dreams." *Association for the Study of Dreams Newsletter* vol. 11, no. 3 (Summer 1994).

Castaneda, Carlos. *Journey to Ixtlan*. New York: Touchstone, 1972.

Ibid., *The Art of Dreaming*. New York: Harper Perennial, 1993.

Gackenbach, Jayne, and Jane Bosveld. *Control Your Dreams*. New York: Harper & Row, 1989.

Garfield, Patricia. *Creative Dreaming*. New York: Ballantine Books, 1974.

Gay, Peter. *Freud: A Life for Our Time*. New York: W.W. Norton & Company, 1988.

Gendlin, Eugene. *Let Your Body Interpret Your Dreams*. Wilmette, IL: Chiron Publications, 1986.

Jung, C. G. "The Archetypes and the Collective Unconscious." In *The Collected Works of C. G. Jung*, vol. 9, Part I, translated by R. F. C. Hull, Bollinger Series XX, Princeton, NJ: Princeton University Press, 1969.

Keleman, Stanley. "The Dream," unpublished work, Berkeley, CA, 1993.

Koch-Sheras, Phyllis R. et al. *Dream On: A Dream Interpretation and Exploration Guide for Women*. Englewood Cliffs, NJ: Prentice-Hall, 1983.

Koch-Sheras, Phyllis R., and Peter Sheras. "Dreams and the Couple: Natural Partners." Paper presented at the Association for Sleep and Dreams Conference, Charlottesville, VA, June 1991.

Mindell, Arnold. *Working on Yourself Alone: Inner Dreambody Work.* New York: Penguin Books, 1990.

Norbu, Namkhai. *Dream Yoga and the Practice of Natural Light.* Ithaca, NY: Snow Lion Publications, 1992.

Perls, Frederick. S. *Gestalt Therapy Verbatim.* New York: Bantam Books, 1971.

Rinpoche, Tenzin W. "Practice of Dream." vol. 1, Audiotape. Richmond, VA: Ligmincha Institute, 1994.

Samuels, Mike, and Nancy Samuels. *Seeing with the Mind's Eye.* New York: Random House, 1975.

Storm, Hyemeyohsts. *Seven Arrows.* New York: Ballantine Books, 1972.

Tart, Charles. *Altered States of Consciousness.* New York: John Wiley & Sons, Inc., 1969.

Van de Castle, Robert. *Our Dreaming Mind.* New York: Ballantine Books, 1994.

CHAPTER 7

Bell, Alison. *The Dream Scene.* Los Angeles: Lowell House, 1994.

Boxer, Sarah. "Inside Our Sleeping Minds." *Modern Maturity* (October–November 1989).

Epel, Naomi. *Writers Dreaming.* New York: Carol Southern Books, 1993.

Faraday, Ann. *Dream Power.* New York: Coward, McCann & Geoghegan, Inc., 1972.

Ibid., *The Dream Game.* New York: Harper & Row Publishers, 1974.

Garfield, Patricia. *Creative Dreaming.* New York: Ballantine Books, 1974.

Graves, Ginny. "Dream On: How to Solve Your Problems while You Sleep." *Mademoiselle* (March 1995).

Harary, Keith. "Language of the Night." *Omni* (September 1993).

Koch-Sheras, Phyllis R. et al. *Dream On: A Dream Interpretation and Exploration Guide for Women.* Englewood Cliffs, NJ: Prentice-Hall, 1983.

Morris, Jill. *The Dream Workbook*. Boston: Little, Brown, and Company, 1985.

Thompson, Charles "Chic." *What A Great Idea!* New York: HarperPerennial, 1992.

Van de Castle, Robert L. *Our Dreaming Mind*. New York: Ballantine Books, 1994.

Von Kreisler, Kristin. "Why We Dream What We Dream." *Reader's Digest* (February 1995).

Windsor, Joan. *Dreams Healing: Expanding the Inner Eye*. New York: Dodd, Mead, & Company, 1987.

CHAPTER 8

Bell, Alison. *The Dream Scene*. Los Angeles: Lowell House, 1994.

Gackenbach, Jayne, and Jane Bosveld. *Control Your Dreams*. New York: Harper & Row Publishers, 1989.

Garfield, Patricia. *Creative Dreaming*. New York: Ballantine Books, 1974.

Koch-Sheras, Phyllis R. et al. *Dream On: A Dream Interpretation and Exploration Guide for Women*. Englewood Cliffs, NJ: Prentice-Hall, 1983.

Ullman, Montague, and Stanley Krippner. *Dream Studies and Telepathy*. New York: Parapsychology Foundation, Inc., 1970.

Ullman, Montague and Nan Zimmerman. *Working with Dreams*, London: Hutchinson and Co., 1979.

Van de Castle, Robert L. *Our Dreaming Mind*. New York: Ballantine Books, 1994.

Virtanen, Leea. *"That Must Have Been ESP!"* Bloomington, IN: Indiana University Press, 1990.

Von Krisler, Kristen. "Why We Dream What We Dream." *Reader's Digest* (February 1995).

CHAPTER 9

Garfield, Patricia. *Your Child's Dreams*. New York: Ballantine Books, 1984.

Jung, Carl S. *Man and His Symbols*. New York: Dell, 1964.

Koch-Sheras, Phyllis R. et al. *Dream On: A Dream Interpretation and Exploration Guide for Women*. Englewood Cliffs, NJ: Prentice-Hall, 1983.

Koch-Sheras, Phyllis R., and Peter Sheras. "Dreams and the Couple: Natural Partners." Paper presented at the Association for Sleep and Dreams Conference, Charlottesville, VA, June 1991.

Signell, Karen. *Wisdom of the Heart: Working with Women's Dreams*. New York: Bantam Books, 1990.

Ullman, Montague, and Nan Zimmerman. *Working with Dreams*. London: Hutchinson and Company, 1979.

INDEX

A

Adler, Alfred, 51, 57–58, 59
Aesclipius, 34
Africa, 37–38, 44
Allen, Steve, 171, 176
Amplification, 130–33
Anima, 55
Animals, 7
Animus, 55
Arabia, ancient, 30–31, 44
Archetype, 54, 91, 133, 166
    and Jung, 80–81, 82–83
Aristotle, 155
Asirinsky, Eugene, 15
Australia (Aborigines), 34

B

Babies, 6
Babylon, 27
Biblical dreams, 28–29
Blake, William, 173

Blind people, 7
Body language, 141–143
Bohr, Niels, 177
Boss, Medard, 67
Buddhism, 26, 40, 155

C

Castaneda, Carlos, 158–159, 160
Catholicism, 29
Chester Beatty Papyrus, 24
Children, 144, 219–223
China, ancient, 33
Christianity, 24, 29, 40
Collective unconscious, 54
Complex, 56
Clairvoyance, 195, 196–197
Clarity dreams, 66–67
Creativity, 171–191

D

Dali, Salvador, 171, 175
Daydream, 3
Devil, 24, 29
Dialoguing, 137–141, 143
Dostoyevsky, Theodor, 173
Drawing, 144–146, 223
Dream:
     definition of, 1, 2
     duration, 9
Dream catcher, 149–50
Dream helper, 81, 91–92, 223
Dream journal, 117–121,
     144, 151
Dream language, 121–125, 130
Dream series, 151–152
Dream shield, 144–148,
     see also Dream Mandala
Dream mandala, 147–148,
     see also Dream Shield
Dream sharing, 212–229
Dream space, 149–150
Dream Yoga, 66–67
Dreamism, 68
Dreamlet, 10
Dzogchen, 66–67, 159–161

E

Egypt (ancient), 25, 32, 40
Einstein, Albert, 171, 177
Electroencephalograph
     (EEG) machine, 15
Erection, 20
Erikson, Erik, 39, 59–60

F

Fantasy, 3, 153, 165–168,
     227–228
Fight-or-flight response, 14, 17
Free association, 49, 130
Freud, Sigmund, 27, 33, 43,
     44, 48–53, 70, 85, 175
     and dream
          interpretation, 71
     and Erikson, 59
     and journals, 116–117
     life of, 52–53
     and symbols, 95
     and visualization, 165

G

Galen, 32
Gawain, Shakti, 166
Gendlin, Eugene, 64–65, 142
Gestalt, 62–63, 72, 121
     and dialoguing, 137–138
Greek, (ancient), 24–26, 27, 33
     authors, 25, 173

H

Hall, Calvin, 60–62, 94
Handel, George F., 176
Healing, 78–79, 163–165, 185
Heart attack, 13
Hebrew, 27
Heraclitus, 210
Herbal dream enhancers, 187
Hinduism, 26, 155
Hitler, Adolph, 194

Hobson, Allan J., 69–72
Homer, 25
Howe, Elias, 176
Huang, Alan, 183
Humanistic psychology, 62
Hypnagogic dreams, 10, 157
Hypnomonic dreams, 10

I

Incubation, 157–158, 168–170,
    178–181, 188–190
Incubus, 33
India (ancient), 34

J

Jacob's Ladder, 26
Jews (ancient),
Journal, *see* Dream Journal
Joyce, James, 173
Jung, Carl, 53–56, 180,
    210, 230
    and archetypes, 80–81,
        82–83, 85
    and dream
        interpretation, 71
    and Freud, 51
    and Hobson, 70
    life of, 56–57
    and visualization, 165

K

Karmic dreams, 66–67
Kekulé von Stadonitz,
    Friederich, 177, 201

Keleman, Stanley, 64, 67, 142
Kleitman, Nathaniel, 15
Koran, the, 30
Krippner, Stanley, 65–66, 199

L

Laberge, Steven, 157–158, 169
Latent content, 50, 59, 61, 129
Leune, Hans Carl, 166
Lucid dreams, 81, 155–165
Lincoln, Abraham, 193
Literature, dream-inspired,
    173–175
Loewi, Otto, 177

M

Manifest content, 50, 59, 129
Masters, Robert, 166
Maury, Alfred, 42
McCartney, Paul, 176
Men, 8
Mesopotamia, 24
Mexico, 34
Mindell, Arnold, 63, 67
Moslems, 30
Muhammad, 30, 43
Music, dream-inspired, 176
Mutual dreams, 195, 197–198
Myclonic jerk, 10

N

Native America, 34, 38
    Sioux, 39
    Iroquois, 39

New Testament, 27
Nicks, Stevie, 176
Nightmares, 4, 11, 78,
    135–136, 219
Night terrors, 5, 220
Nocturnal hallucinations,
    203–205
Norbu, Namkhai, 160–162

O

Old Testament, 26–27
Oneirocritica, 25
Oneiros, 25
Oneirocritics, 43
"Out-of-body" experiences,
    202–203

P

Paranormal dreams, 194
Percept language, 121
Perls, Fritz, xvi, 60, 62–63, 83
    and dialoguing, 137–138
Phoenecia, 27
Poe, Edgar Allan, 174
Practice of the Night,
    160–161
Precognitive dreams,
    200–202
Psi dreams, 194
    experiments with,
    205–208
Psychic phenomena, 194
Psychoanalysis, 48–52
Pregnancy, 104

R

Recurring dreams, 81, 151
Rapid Eye Movement
    (REM), 14–16, 159, 169
Reed, Henry, 170
Rice, Anne, 171, 174
Rinpoche, Tenzin, 161–162

S

Scientific discoveries,
    dream-inspired, 176
Soul travels, 32
Sleepwalking, 11, 19
Sleep cycle, 14, 16, 18
    and bodily changes, 19
Sufism, 26
Sumeria, 24, 43
Sunnis, the, 30
Synesius of Cyrene, 27

T

Taczo, Alberto, 67
Talmud, the, 27, 32, 33, 44
Tan, Amy, 174
Taoism, 26, 155
Tart, Charles, 155
Telepathy, 195, 197
Temenos, 210
Tholey, Paul, 158, 160
Thompson, Charles "Chic,"
    183–185
Titanic, the, 193

U

Ullman, Montague, 68, 194, 224
Unconscious, 49–51, 69

V

Van Eeden, Frederick, 155
Visualization, 165–166,
    see also Fantasy
Van de Castle, Robert, 61, 169
Voltaire, 173

W

Wagner, Richard, 176
Waking dream, 3
Weir, John, xvii, 67, 121–122
Winson, Jonathan, 70–71
Wolpe, Joseph, 166
Women, 8